The church must carefully guard its
by establishing high standards for th
ministry of pastor. It is the church's responsibility to carefully
limit the ordained ministry to those who are properly called,
gifted and trained. The Apostle Paul expected special honor to
be given those elders who preach and teach precisely because the
health and witness of the church depends so heavily upon those
entrusted with its public ministry. For years Terry Johnson has
called the Reformed church to remember and return to her rich
liturgical heritage. In this fine book Pastor Johnson focuses on
the pastor's role in leading the church in worship. The pastor is
not one who merely appears in time to preach on Sundays. The
pastor is one chiefly entrusted with leading the church in praise
and prayer. Not only will pastors be helped by this excellent little
book but so too will sessions and church members who may need
reminding what precisely it is that pastors are called and ordained
to do.

TODD PRUITT
Pastor, Covenant Presbyterian Church
Harrisonburg, Virgina

*The Pastor's Public Ministry* is important for the questions it
raises, the balance it strikes and for the rich guidance Terry
Johnson offers in the conduct of public worship. It's both the
kind of book that every seminary student should read before
beginning his ministry and a ready reminder to serving
pastors of the deep significance of what they do every Lord's
Day in leading people in their corporate engagement with
God. For Johnson, no part of corporate worship should simply
be assumed. Rather, each component (praise, prayer, Scripture
reading and preaching) deserves thorough assessment, careful
planning and thoughtful conduct to the end that God's
people worship with a consciousness that they are at "the gate
of Heaven".

IVER MARTIN
Principal, Edinburgh Theological Seminary, Edinburgh UK

As an active minister for well over fifty years, I have read much in order to focus my presentation of Christ to those who need him and I have read much about how to preach – and I am still seeking to learn more. But I have read much less about prayer and worship. Terry Johnson's book, *The Pastor's Public Ministry*, is one of the better meditations on how to lead a congregation in worship and prayer. He deals with the most serious issues clearly, helping us find the way forward to praise the Lord and edify the people. Johnson offers some of the most practical advice anywhere on public prayer, rightly noting that very little has been written on it in the last 100 years. I particularly appreciated his emphasis on how public prayer should utilize the language of Scripture, noting that one ought no more to pray without preparation than to preach without preparation. I sincerely believe his chapter on this topic will help you move in that direction. We greatly need this book.

Douglas F. Kelly
Professor Emeritus, Reformed Theological Seminary
Charlotte, North Carolina

I have long sought a concise and insightful guide on this vital subject, one I could confidently place in the hands of a young seminary student or minister of the gospel to steer them back to the simplicity, profundity, and beauty of biblical, experiential, and well-ordered worship services. At last, the search is over. Terry Johnson has done it again. Brief, clear, and brimming with practical wisdom gleaned from nearly 40 years of ordained ministry, this resource is unparalleled. It is not just a book but a guide, the perfect tool to equip a young minister tasked with the profound responsibility of leading the church, Lord's Day by Lord's Day, before the presence of Almighty God in worship.

Neil Stewart
Senior Minister, First Presbyterian Church
Columbia, South Carolina

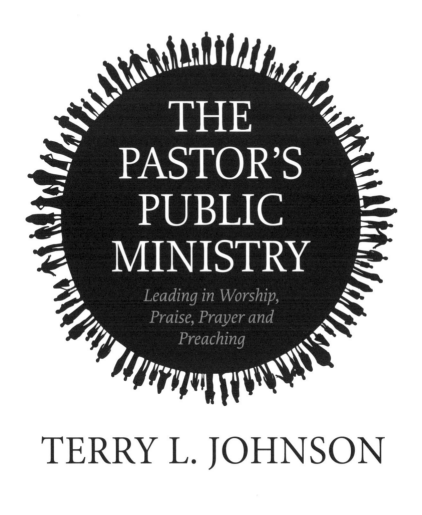

# THE PASTOR'S PUBLIC MINISTRY

*Leading in Worship,
Praise, Prayer and
Preaching*

# TERRY L. JOHNSON

CHRISTIAN
FOCUS

Copyright © Terry L. Johnson 2024

paperback ISBN 978-1-5271-1164-6
ebook ISBN 978-1-5271-1238-4

10 9 8 7 6 5 4 3 2 1

Published in 2024
by
Christian Focus Publications Ltd.,
Geanies House, Fearn, Ross-shire
IV20 1TW, Great Britain.

www.christianfocus.com

Cover design by Rubner Durais

Printed and bound by
Bell and Bain Glasgow

MIX
Paper | Supporting
responsible forestry
FSC
www.fsc.org
FSC® C007785

# Contents

# Foreword

It has become proverbial, at least since David Wells drew our attention to it, that ministers in our age are expected to be jacks-of-all-trades. Numerous responsibilities vie for their attention. Many of these activities, however, bear little relation to the central duties of their calling.

Administration, committee work, counseling, relationship building (not to say historic pastoral visitation of the more robust sort), public relations and a variety of other activities compete with a focus on the ministry of the Word. And these pressures impact not only preparation for the preaching of God's Word, but also (and perhaps especially) preparation of and for public worship. Add to this the fact that ministers often lack the training for and experience of (and sometimes even the inclination to be interested in) historic worship, expository preaching, and pulpit prayer, and it is easy to see why the general conduct of public pastoral ministry is a real challenge for younger ministers.

This situation is one reason I am so delighted to introduce and commend this book to you. I know of no one in the Presbyterian Church in America more graciously committed to and knowledgeable about historic Presbyterian worship than Terry Johnson. He is "our" Hughes Old. And in this book, Johnson turns his attention to three important matters in the conduct of the pastor's public ministry: ministerial leadership in worship, public prayer, and preaching.

One problem, evident in the corporate praise of many congregations, is a lack of ministerial leadership in worship. Ministers are often, willing or unwillingly, uninvolved in vital aspects of worship planning. Indeed, worship planning is often left to "worship teams," leaders, and committees. This is illustrated in the content of one trendy, glossy magazine devoted to the subject of the conduct of public worship. A friend of mine recently observed that the articles are clearly designed, not for ministers, but rather for the mysterious being now known as the "worship leader." It is simply assumed that the minister will not be leading in worship. This is a tragedy and Terry Johnson will tell you why and offer a biblical corrective in the first section of this pithy book.

A second matter that confronts us is that of public prayer. No aspect of contemporary American Reformed church practice more strikingly illustrates our impoverishment in worship than does our weakness in pastoral prayer. In many services it is all but absent. In multi-staff churches, it is farmed out to an assistant. In most cases it is extremely brief, bereft of gravitas, and relegated to an invocation and offertory petition. There is little confession, assurance of pardon, thanksgiving, or general supplication to be found in many pastoral prayers.

What is the answer to such a situation? Not a book of common prayer, as some might suggest. No, the best of the Reformed tradition has avoided a diet of read prayers (especially when they have been written by others in "prefab" prayer books) and has instead espoused the practice of studied pastoral prayer. That is, the minister devotes himself to preparation for prayer (as he would his sermon) and wills his prayers with the language of Scripture.

Furthermore, a sense of the singular importance of ministerial public prayer must be recaptured by the minister himself. C. H. Spurgeon once commented on the vital significance of the pastoral prayer by saying that if he had to choose between preaching the sermon and praying the pastoral prayer, he reckoned that the sermon would just have to go! This, from a man who in no way denigrated the centrality of the pulpit, speaks volumes to us regarding the urgency of recovering robust pastoral prayer.

Terry Johnson understands all this, and, in the second section of the book, he leads you in a helpful treatment of resources for and principles of public pulpit prayer. If we pay heed to him, we will strengthen our weaknesses in prayer in worship.

A third area addressed in this volume is preaching – expository preaching. Now, sad to say, we live in a day of "preaching wars" just as we live in a day of "worship wars." On the one hand, many have decided that expository preaching, preaching anchored in the text of Scripture that seeks to expound its meaning for the congregation, will not work. They have lost confidence in this method of preaching. Oh, they claim still to believe the message, but the methods, they say, need some updating. Drama, video clips, skits, dance, and other contextualized modes of communication are all the rage in some quarters!

On the other hand, even among those who profess to believe in expository preaching, there are major disagreements as to how it should be done. Some believe only in preaching short series and eschew *lectio continua* preaching (the exposition of whole Bible books, verse by verse, chapter by chapter). Others say that the sermon must always begin with "where the audience is." Still others opine that every sermon must end on a note of grace (even a message on Hebrews 6:1-8) while others view any application as a sin and judiciously guard against what they call "moralizing." *What's a preacher to do?*

Never fear, Terry Johnson has come to our rescue with sound advice and specific recommendations on our practice of expository preaching. His suggestions are sane and biblical, and reflective of a man with many years of pastoral experience. Read them and benefit.

A prayerful reading of this book may result in a real improvement in your conduct of public ministry and thus prove of great aid to your congregation's approach to God. Above all, may God's glory be served as you read, mark, and learn from this vintage teaching on pastoral ministry.

LIGON DUNCAN
Chancellor
Reformed Theological Seminary

# Preface

In the same way that *Reformed Worship*[1] expanded and grew to become *Worshipping with Calvin*,[2] so also The Pastor's Public Ministry expanded to become *Serving with Calvin*.[3] As *Reformed Worship* now functions as an introduction to the *Worshipping with Calvin*'s more detailed and documented treatment of the theology and history behind Reformed worship, so likewise we now offer to the public *The Pastor's Public Ministry* as an introduction to *Serving with Calvin*'s extended treatment of how to implement the principles of Reformed worship.

*The Pastor's Public Ministry* began as the Den Dulk Lectures at Westminster Theological Seminary in California, February 25-27, 1997. The lectures became a pair of articles published in the *Westminster Theological Journal*,[4] and finally, a booklet published by Reformed Academic Press in 2001. We have lightly revised the content and repackaged it for use today. The issues that prompted writing on these themes twenty-five years ago remain with us still today.

---

1  Terry L. Johnson, *Reformed Worship* (Darlington: EP Books, 2010).

2  Terry L. Johnson, *Worshipping with Calvin* (Darlington: EP Books, 2014).

3  Terry L. Johnson, *Serving with Calvin* (Darlington: EP Books, 2015).

4  Terry L. Johnson, "The Pastor's Public Ministry: Part One," *Westminster Theological Journal*, 60 (1998), 131-152; "The Pastor's Public Ministry: Conclusion," *Westminster Theological Journal*, 60 (1998), 297-325.

# Introduction

# The Pastor's Public Ministry[1]

What is the meaning of the traditional process by which ministers are ordained? For example, why do Presbyterians and Reformed churches require a long and painful process involving the care of session, care of presbytery, three years of theological education, internship, call, oral and written presbytery exams, and, finally, ordination? The Reformed churches have always emphasized the need for a "learned clergy," but not as an end in itself. Why then must ministers be so carefully trained and so thoroughly examined? We can find no chapter and verse that says that it must be done this way. Indeed, some other traditions don't. Allow me to interpret our practice for us: the church is fulfilling its responsibility to "guard the gospel" (1 Tim. 6:20; 2 Tim. 1:13-14). By limiting the public ministry of the church to those called, gifted, and prepared to do so, it is protecting the gospel from the theological errors of the untrained and the moral failures of the unexamined. It is especially the public ministry about which the church is concerned.

The public ministry has been carefully guarded by the church from the very beginning. Recall the foundational texts upon

---

1 What follows in the next fifty-four pages is considered at much greater depth in Johnson, *Worshipping with Calvin* and *Serving with Calvin*.

which is built our understanding of the offices of the church. Acts 6 records a dispute concerning the serving of meals to Hellenistic and Palestinian Jewish Christian widows. Men were chosen to perform this very public function. It was required that they be of good reputation, full of the Holy Spirit and of wisdom (v.3), elected by the congregation (v.5), and set apart, or ordained, by prayer and the imposition of hands (v.6). This, mind you, was for the purpose of waiting on tables. Contemplate the meaning of this for future generations. The apostolic church was guarding the gospel by guarding its public ministry, limiting participation in it to proven men.

Is this not also the meaning of the long lists of character and conduct requirements found in 1 Timothy 3 and Titus 1? Elders and deacons are to be men observed over a period of time sufficient to prove their character and demonstrate their knowledge and conduct. They must not be novices or recent converts. Elders must be "able to teach," even "exhort in sound doctrine" and "refute those who contradict" it (1 Tim. 3:2; Titus 1:9). Likewise, deacons must be "full of wisdom," which implies considerable knowledge of the Scriptures from which one gains wisdom. Holding a public office of the church requires the highest standards of knowledge, character and conduct. The New Testament in general and the Pastoral Epistles in particular repeatedly and emphatically require that we "guard what has been entrusted" to us (1 Tim. 5:20, 2 Tim. 1:14, 2:15, 3:14, 4:1-5, etc.). The church must not lay hands on anyone "hastily" (2 Tim. 5:22). The gospel is guarded by requiring of those who enter the church's public offices a long period of observation followed by careful examination.

If this is true of the church's "lay" leadership, what then can we say about those responsible for the ministry of the Word and sacraments? The distinction between elders who "rule well" and those who "labor at preaching and teaching," is found in

1 Tim 5:17. The charge to "give attention to the public reading of Scripture, to exhortation, and teaching" is directly related to the command to "not neglect the spiritual gift within you, which was bestowed upon you through prophetic utterance with the laying on of hands by the presbytery" (1 Tim. 4:13-14 NASB). From the beginning, the church has seen it as a matter of good order that even higher standards be required of those who regularly conduct public worship, preach and administer the sacraments than are required of other elders and deacons. The setting apart of a presbyter, a presiding elder, from among the presbyters, who was responsible for the ministry of the Word and Sacraments, yet was still subject to the presbyters as a whole can be found among the oldest extra-biblical documents, including those dating from the first and second centuries.[2] "The things which you have heard from me," Paul tells Timothy, "these entrust to faithful men, who will be able to teach others also" (2 Tim. 2:2).

The long, careful, process of identifying, educating, examining, calling and ordaining ministers has as its goal ensuring that those who conduct public worship, administer the sacraments and preach are qualified and equipped to do so. Our age exerts enormous egalitarian pressure on the church. These pressures, in combination with the ministry of every member described in Romans 12 and 1 Corinthians 12, have worked to obscure the distinctive call of the minister. We shall say more about this later. Suffice it for now to say that Christ has given "pastors and teachers" to the church to equip the saints for the work of ministry (Eph. 4:11-12). The work of the "saints" depends upon the faithful labors of those with the word gifts, the pastors and teachers. Their work is public and official, that of the "laity" is private and informal. Ministers are called, trained, examined and ordained in particular to conduct the public ministry of

---

2 T. M. Lindsey, *The Church and Its Ministry in the Early Centuries* (London: Hodder and Stoughton, 1903), 170ff.

the church. We repeat: the church, by requiring this, guards its gospel from the theological errors of the uninformed, and the moral lapses of the unexamined.

# 1

# Leading in Worship[1]

The Reformation was not only a theological revolution, but also a liturgical revolution. One might accurately say it was a theological-driven liturgical revolution. It restored the worship forms of the patristic church, and, in doing so, revolutionized the preaching, praying, singing, Scripture reading, and sacramental practices of the medieval and renaissance church. Worship was ranked by Calvin and his successors in importance alongside the doctrine of justification by faith as vital and necessary reforms of the church.[2]

## FIRST PRIORITY

The most basic and essential task of the minister is that of leading public worship. Worship is also the highest priority of the church. A moment's reflection will confirm the accuracy of

---

1 For a complete guide to leading worship services, see T. L. Johnson, *Leading in Worship* (1996; Durham, UK: EP Books, 2019), a handbook for ministers, with sections on regular services (Sunday morning and evening), occasional services (baptisms, weddings, funerals, etc.), seasonal services (Christmas, Easter, etc.), and historical examples (Calvin's "Form," Knox's "Form," the Westminster Assembly's "Directory," etc.).

2 As Calvin argued in his famous essay "On the Necessity of Reforming the Church," in *Selected Works of John Calvin*, Vol. 1. (1844, Grand Rapids: Baker Book House, 1983), 1:226.

these statements. Worship is our first calling (Rom. 1:18ff) and our ultimate purpose (John 4:21ff; Rom. 11:33-36).[3] "Worship is the most high and honorable of all our works," says the Puritan George Swinnock (1627–73).[4] Moreover, it is primarily in the public services of worship that the means of grace are operative. Here, the gospel is preached and the sacraments are administered. As for prayer, though prayers may be offered in one's closet (Matt. 6:1ff), let us not forget the special promise of Jesus concerning prayers offered where "two or three have gathered in My name," likely a reference to organized public worship (Matt. 18:15-20). Of such prayers He says, "If two of you agree on earth about anything that they may ask, it will be done for them by My Father who is in heaven." There is a unique efficacy in the public prayers of the church.

This is not to depreciate the private or individual side of the ministry. Counseling and discipleship, administration and management, leadership training and fund raising all have their part. However, these tasks are secondary to and dependent upon the public services of the church. Only as the public ministry of the Word and Sacraments flourishes can there be a sufficient foundation for private ministries. Without it, there will be few to counsel or disciple, little to administer or manage, and few to train. The church's assessment of a pastor's ministry will primarily be based on his public preaching. That claim may seem a bit far-fetched and more than a bit unfair. Nevertheless, it is true. The pastor is who he is *as a preacher* to most of the congregation. Among contemporary writers, William H. Willimon puts it this way:

> While we do not deny the importance of all the things we do, there is one role we must do and do well or we are in big trouble.

---

3 Johnson, *Reformed Worship,* 23-29.

4 George Swinnock, "The Incomparableness of God," in *The Works of George Swinnock,* Vols. 1-5 (1868; Edinburgh, UK: The Banner of Truth Trust, 1992), IV:503.

> If our time and talent are not heavily invested in the tasks of preaching and worship leadership, our congregations are correct in assuming that we have lost the central focus of our ministry.[5]

We have found it necessary repeatedly to redirect the prayers of our morning men's prayer meeting so that participants would focus on the regular, ongoing public ministry of the church. For years, their prayers have been relatively exotic (Aunt Mabel's hiatal hernia) while neglecting prayer for the Sunday and Wednesday services into which we pour the bulk of our energies, time, and resources. We build and maintain buildings; we hire support staff, musicians, and ministers; we pay utility bills, print bulletins, and maintain a nursery all for the sake of what? The overwhelming amount of the church's time, energy, and resources is directly or indirectly related to the stated meetings of the church. Even the church's benevolence or missions budget is only possible because of the "success" or failure of the public services. The church's ability to raise the revenues necessary to support the church's work at home and abroad is directly dependent on the popularity and success (meaning these in their best sense) of its regular services of worship.

Given that these things are so, given that leading public worship is the minister's primary calling, this means that public worship is not only the most important but the most fruitful of all his activities. It is dismaying to observe the prevailing mindlessness of most of what passes for worship, with the exception of the sermon. Most of the ministers in evangelical circles seem to work hard at their sermons. Yet few, it appears, give much thought to anything else. There is usually little discernable logic, flow, or pace to the average service. Seldom does there seem to be much of a rationale for the hymn selection.

---

5 William H. Willimon, *Preaching and Leading Worship* (Philadelphia: The Westminster Press, 1984), 9.

Rarely can one discern any planning behind the content of the prayers, most ministers, one imagines, praying whatever happens to pop into their minds. Transitions between elements have the "and now, this!" quality found on television variety shows, where, in fact, there is no connection between what went before and what comes after. One is reminded of the Puritan complaint against the Anglican liturgy that it seemed to throw in this or that item "like tennis balls." Things seem to be plugged in here and there without any apparent reason, other than to fill up the time slot. Elements seem to be dropped or added without regard for Scripture or tradition or logic.

The result is largely incoherent and unattractive worship services. It doesn't seem to matter if the services are "traditional" or "contemporary." The former are often criticized for being boring, and with some justification. Indeed, they sometimes are dull, slow, and devoid of any obvious coherence. Likewise, the latter are often criticized for being shallow, aesthetically embarrassing (both for the quality of the music and the quality of the words), and intellectually dissatisfying. There is no lack of evidence that this judgment is largely justified as well. We see no future for the kind of worship that is now prevalent. The key to reform lies with the "clergy" and the kind of leadership that they will give to tomorrow's worship. How will tomorrow's ministers preach? How will they pray? How will they administer the sacraments and lead the church's public services? The answers we give affect the future health and fruitfulness of the church's ministry: No less is at stake.

## PRINCIPLES OF WORSHIP LEADERSHIP

Since worship is our ultimate priority and since public worship is the primary context where means of grace are operative, we therefore recommend the following seven principles.

**Worship services**

First, lead public worship services that are *services of worship.*
I was reared in churches in the Los Angeles area that were of
the revivalistic tradition. Our worship services looked like
evangelistic crusades, complete with first and last stanzas of
numerous gospel songs, special music, little prayer or Scripture
reading, an evangelistic sermon, altar call, and multiple verses of
"Just As I Am." My college years were spent at the University of
Southern California, where I became involved in various campus
ministries. Through their influence, the revivalistic format was
supplanted by the contemporary, with gospel songs giving way to
Scripture choruses, overtly evangelistic sermons to Bible studies,
and altar calls to the "Four Spiritual Laws." Upon graduation
I traveled to England, embarking on a two-year study of theology
at Trinity College, Bristol, an Anglican theological college. Daily
chapel was required and, of course, we worshiped with the Prayer
Book. I am embarrassed to say that for six months I hated it.
When told that only 3 to 10 percent of the English population
was in church on Sunday I thought, "And no wonder!" But then,
one day, the thought came to me that had never occurred to me in
my previous twenty-two years of church going. The constant use
of the Prayer Book had finally made one huge overall impression:
that *one goes to church in order to worship God.* I had understood
that one goes to church to evangelize the lost; or to hear the
Bible taught; or to enjoy the fellowship of the saints; or to enjoy
the music. Church service as either revival, or lecture, or social
gathering, or concert, or even as therapy had been my bias at one
time or another. But as worship? This was a new thought. This
is not to say that these other things do not occur in the context
of worship. Evangelism, teaching, fellowship, singing all occur in
the worship of the church. However, they are not *the* purpose for
our gathering. Only worship can provide the ultimate rationale
for our services.

The many questions about what one should or should not do in worship may easily be answered by asking the question, is it worship? The consideration is not do the people like it, or does it make them feel good, or is it popular? Rather one should ask, *is a given activity a legitimate element of the church's collective devotional life?* Does it give expression to the people's praise of God or demonstrate their submission to His revealed will? If not, eliminate it. If so, there are still a few questions to ask, but one is well on the way to having a final answer.

At the church I serve, we have very different settings in which we worship. In the morning, we meet in a nearly perfect example of Protestant architecture on a grand scale. Complete with a fourteen-foot-high solid mahogany "high pulpit," it is one of the most beautiful houses of worship in North America. In the summer, we travel a few miles down the road to a camp facility where we have a very informal service in what looks like a camp lodge. A few years back we became so informal in that setting, with hymn requests, prayer requests, a "light and lively" atmosphere, that I judged that the services were close to losing their integrity as *worship* services. Today, these services are still informal, in that we sit in removable chairs, we dress casually, and I preach more dialogically. Yet with an opening prayer of praise that is lengthy and weighty, with the reading of the law and a confession of sin, with a distinct prayer of intercession, the service is once again clearly a service of worship, with the "reverence and awe" that is to characterize our praise (Heb. 12:28).

Perhaps one takes the view that the church's public gatherings are more than times of worship. Perhaps one is convinced that they ought also be times for "sharing," conducting some church business or transmitting information. If so (though I don't grant the point), then still one ought to differentiate between worship per se and these other activities. For example, announcements can be given before the call to worship. If the congregation wants a "hymn sing," this can be done before the service starts. Business meetings can be held after the benediction. In this way, the integrity of the church's collective devotional life is not undermined by distracting activity.

## Public services

Second, lead the worship services of the church that are services of *public* worship. By this we mean that the services should clearly be public not private, collective not individualistic, and congregational not personal. There is no need to cater to the needs of individual and personal devotion in public worship. This we take to be true by definition. It is necessary in the nature of things, by definition, in a public service for the individual to subordinate his immediate state of mind to the requirements of group expression. A person may not "feel" like God is "Holy, Holy, Holy," but he praises Him as such anyway. He may not feel like confessing his sin or confessing his faith that day. Yet he rightly joins in because these are public, congregational, corporate exercises, expressing the convictions of the community as a whole. Of course, it ought to be the aim of every worshiper for his heart to match his mouth. However, in the meantime, by faith he adopts the public language. Without this step of faith, public worship becomes impossible, as each individual searches for language which more perfectly expresses the condition of his own heart. Public worship does not collapse into an anarchy of individual expression because hymns, Psalms, creeds, and public prayers express what *we* believe and aspire to be.

So then, the *exercises* of public worship services are *collective and congregational.* There is a tendency to add to public worship moments for silent and personal prayer, moments for personal confession, and moments for personal intercession. We see this as being entirely unnecessary, even contrary to the nature of the service as a public service. If it is necessary to add such activities in order to encourage "personal participation," what are we to make of the rest of the service? Is the congregation not participating during the minister's prayers and preaching or during congregational responses such as songs and creeds? *All of the activities of public worship should be public and congregational in nature.*

In addition, because the services are public, its *concerns* are public. Richard J. Mouw, President of Fuller Theological Seminary complains about preachers who "seem convinced that I have come to church eager to be updated about their daily lives."[6] The intimacy and informality that may be appropriate to private devotions or family worship are often unsuitable for services that are public. You may wear your pajamas for personal devotions, yet they are not advised for public. You may ask questions about the Bible of your four-year-old during family worship, yet such is unlikely to be edifying during public worship, however cute it may be. In a house church or small group setting it may be appropriate to take personal prayer requests, to confess particular sins, to have personal testimonies. However, once a gathering increases in number beyond a half-dozen or so, matters must be handled in a more generalized way. Otherwise the congregation risks becoming cliquish. Intercessions should be of a general nature, as should the confession of sin, as should the confession of faith, or else the congregation will quickly divide into the in-group whose needs and experiences are known and voiced, and all the rest. There is an informality or familiarity that is inappropriate for public gatherings. Maintain the measure of formality that is suited to services that are public.

**Well-ordered services**

Third, *order* the public services of the church by the *principle of "gospel logic"* i.e., a logical and experiential order in our approach

---

6  Richard J. Mouw, "Preaching Worth Pondering," *Fuller Focus* 5 (November 1996) 2,3.

to God. The worship of God begins with the praise of God. We "enter His gates with thanksgiving, and His courts with praise" (Ps. 100:4; see also Ps. 95:2). "Praise is the gateway to God's presence," says Hughes Old.[7] On this point Scripture, the historic liturgies, and recent aids to popular piety all agree. Jesus taught us to begin our prayers with praise: "Our Father, who art in heaven, hallowed be Thy name. Thy kingdom come, Thy will be done, on earth as it is in heaven." Jesus praises God's name, stature, holiness, and work before He offers any petitions. The Psalms which are classified as hymns of praise, and are believed to have been intended primarily for use in public worship (and often indicate such themselves) all begin with a call to worship.[8] The historic Protestant liturgies, including the Westminster Assembly's *Directory for Public Worship,* all begin with a "Call to Worship" or invocation. Matthew Henry (1662–1714), in *A Method for Prayer*, identifies "the first part of prayer" as adoration and praise, and Isaac Watts (1674–1748), in *A Guide to Prayer*, identifies it as "invocation, or calling upon God," and the "second part" as adoration.[9] Today's popular aids to prayer such as the acrostic A-C-T-S, Adoration-Confession-Thanksgiving-Supplication, or the three P's, Praise-Pardon-Petition, likewise guide one to approach God with praise. Indeed, this is the pattern of conversion: We come to Christ only when we begin to understand God and what He requires of us. For these reasons, we counsel that one begin worship with what might be called a "cycle of praise." We do not see this as an absolute, nor do we see

---

7  Hughes O. Old, "The Psalms as Christian Prayer, A Preface to the Liturgical Use of the Psalter," unpublished manuscript, 1978, 86.

8  Such as Psalms 8, 19, 29, 33, 46, 48, 65, 66, 93, 96, 97, 98, 99, 100, 104, 111, 113, 114, 117, 135, 136, and 145-150.

9  Matthew Henry, *A Method for Prayer,* ed. J. Ligon Duncan, III (1710; Fearn, Ross-Shire: Christian Heritage, 1994); Isaac Watts, *A Guide to Prayer* (1715; Edinburgh; The Banner of Truth Trust, 2001).

any item in the cycle as unalterable. Yet it is a sensible, logical beginning to worship, and frankly, we fail to see any better.

> **Cycle of Praise**
> > Call to Worship
> > Invocation and Prayer of Praise
> > Psalm\Hymn of Praise[10]
> > Confession of Faith
> > Gloria Patri\Doxology

The praise of God may then be followed by the confession of sin. Repeatedly in the Scripture, a vision of the true God leads to fear and awe and a sense of one's finiteness, sin, and unworthiness. Moses, after viewing the "backsides" of God's glory, "made haste to bow low toward the earth and worship" (Ex. 34:8 NASB); Isaiah responds to the vision of the Lord of hosts upon His throne, surrounded by Seraphim, by crying out, "Woe is me, for I am ruined! Because I am a man of unclean lips, and I live among a people of unclean lips; for my eyes have seen the King, the Lord of hosts" (Isa. 6:5 NASB). Peter, after Jesus performs a miracle, becomes aware of the One with whom he is dealing and calls out, "Depart from me for I am a sinful man" (Luke 5:8). Seeing a vision of Christ on His throne in heaven, John writes, "And when I saw Him, I fell at His feet as a dead man" (Rev. 1:17 NASB). A true knowledge of God leads to a knowledge of ourselves, and the new self-awareness is humbling. No one ever stated this better than Calvin:

> It is certain that man never achieves a clear knowledge of himself unless he has first looked upon God's face, and then

---

10 "The first hymn should be one of general praise, serving to inspire feelings of worship and adoration towards God" says W.G.T. Shedd, in *Homiletics and Pastoral Theology,* (1867; reprint, Edinburgh: The Banner of Truth Trust, 1965), 270. It should be "emphatically a hymn of worship," says Broadus, *On the Preparation and Delivery of Sermons,* (1870; reprint, Nashville: Broadman Press, 1944), 365.

descends from contemplating him to scrutinize himself … As a consequence, we must infer that man is never sufficiently touched and affected by the awareness of his lowly state until he has compared himself with God's majesty.[11]

Consequently, we recommend that the cycle of praise be followed by a cycle of confession. American Presbyterianism has not made widespread liturgical use of the Ten Commandments. The experience of using them on Reformation Sunday (with liturgies of Knox, Calvin, and Baxter) was so positive that our church began to use them on a weekly basis on Sunday nights. We highly commend them as a prelude to confession. This cycle gives a gravity and weightiness that is typically lacking in modern worship, providing an effective antidote to the trivialities of our day. Confession of sin also clears the way for God's blessing, removing from our hearts whatever idols or lusts are obstructing the grace of God (see Isa. 59:2; Ps. 66:18). A cycle of confession might look like this:

**Cycle of Confession**
>Reading of the Law of God
>Confession of Sin
>Assurance of Pardon
>Psalm\Hymn of Thanksgiving

From here, the service moves into a cycle employing the means of grace. Those who have contemplated God have been illuminated by the light of His glory. They have repented of their sin, trusted Christ, and now are ready to grow in their faith. When we know our need of grace, we make use of the means of grace. This progression should not be viewed negatively as a "reenactment

---

11 John Calvin, *Institutes of the Christian Religion*, 2 vols., ed. John T. McNeill, trans. Ford Lewis Battles, The Library of Christian Classics (1559; Philadelphia: Westminster Press, 1960), 68-69.

of redemption," which for some may imply that Christ's work is incomplete and requires regular repeating.[12] Instead, it flows from our daily experience with Christ as well as the logic of a public approach to God. To begin worship with the means of grace, say, with an intercessory shopping list, without first having paid homage to God and confessed our sins is inappropriately self-centered. Yet having praised and confessed, we humbly turn to the Scriptures, read and preached, to prayer, and to the sacraments for the grace that is necessary to sustain the Christian life.

### Cycle Employing the Means of Grace
> Prayer of Illumination
> Reading of Scripture
> Sermon
> Prayers of Intercession
> Sacraments

The service then concludes with a response of thanksgiving and blessing. This includes the collection of an offering as an expression of gratitude for our redemption.

### Cycle of Thanksgiving and Blessing
> Exhortation to Give or Prayer for Giving
> Collection
> Concluding hymn[13]
> Benediction

Again, let us underscore that neither the order nor the items under each cycle is absolute and unalterable. For example, the

---

12 John Frame, *Worship in Spirit and Truth* (Phillipsburg, N.J.: Presbyterian and Reformed Publishers, 1996), 68-69.

13 The final hymn "should ... refer to the discourse ... being didactic and applicatory of the sermon," Shedd, *Homiletics,* 270, 271.

collection can be justified at just about any point in the service: as an opening declaration of Christ's Lordship; as a response to forgiveness; as a response to the sermon, or dropped all together.[14] Sins may be confessed without the Law. Indeed, the prayers of confession and intercession may be combined into one "great prayer," as in the American low-church Protestant tradition. There is room for considerable variation. Yet this basic outline provides a worship service with the logic, order, and flow that is often missing in today's worship. It does so in a way that is consistent with scriptural example, with Christian experience, and the Reformed tradition.

### Reverent services

Fourth, *establish an atmosphere of reverence.* Those who attend our services ought to sense that they are meeting with God. Like the unbeliever who visited the early Corinthian assembly, they should overhear such convicting preaching (or "prophesy"), and observe such zealous devotion that they are "convicted by all … called to account by all; the secrets of [their] heart[s] are disclosed; and so [they] will fall on [their] face[s] and worship God, declaring that God is certainly among you" (1 Cor. 14:25). Such serious, soul-searching proclamation is not, by the way, terribly seeker-friendly. Instead, the visitor is "convicted;" he is "called to account," and "the secrets of his heart are disclosed." That this might make him uncomfortable does not seem to have concerned the apostle. Indeed, that is the intention. The result is conversion, leading to strong acts of devotion, whether literal or figurative. He will "fall on his face and worship God," presumably joining with the others in worshiping God. It is clear even to the unbeliever who visits the Christian assembly that the people are dealing with God and God is dealing with them.

---

14  For the argument that the "offering" is appropriate but not necessary, see Robert Godfrey, "The Offering," *The Outlook,* 41 (Nov. 1991).

Westminster Professor Edmund Clowney (1917–2005) has called this "doxological evangelism." Authentically God-centered worship makes a positive evangelistic impact.

We are compelled to ask: is this sense of reverence in most of our churches today? The light, superficial, frivolous atmosphere of many churches today creates quite the opposite impression, does it not? Whatever these Christians are doing, the unbeliever might conclude, they are not dealing with Almighty God! They are enjoying themselves. The man up front is charming. The musicians are entertaining. But meeting with God? Is the unbeliever typically concluding, "God is certainly among you"? Rarely, if ever, we fear. Yet surely this is the way things ought to be. After all, we are commanded to worship "with reverence and awe" (Heb. 12:28). We take this to mean that reverence and awe are mandatory. Both the devotion of the congregation and the leadership of the minister ought to be convicting of divine realities. For this to happen, the minister is the key. Therefore, we recommend he do the following to promote a reverential atmosphere.

*1. Encourage preparation for worship.*
The Psalms of Ascent (Ps. 24, 67, 84, and especially 120–134), originally used by pilgrims as they approached and then entered the Temple in Jerusalem, stand as testimonies to the importance of preparation for worship. Teach the congregation to begin preparing on Saturday night to meet with God in public worship on Sunday morning. Advise them to conclude secular obligations and to set one's affairs in order. Teach them to observe the Lord's Day as a Christian Sabbath, devoted in its entirety to worship and "holy rest." Encourage them to arrive for worship early, and revive the Presbyterian custom of praying immediately upon taking one's seat. Urge them to silently read the Psalms of Ascent, contemplating both their praise and penitential qualities. Perhaps

have the musical instruments play familiar hymns or have the congregation sing them as they gather. In order to protect the integrity of the worship service, give the announcements at this time and limit them to three or four, and perhaps even restrict them to those which pertain only to the whole congregation.[15] This encourages a "cycle of preparation" prior to the call to worship that aids in establishing an atmosphere of reverence.

**Cycle of Preparation**
    Ongoing Sabbath Teaching
    Silent Prayer Upon Seating
    Instrumental Music or Quiet Singing
    Announcements

*2. Adopt a sober, serious tone.*
Why? Because the people of God have assembled to *worship*. Because we are commanded to worship God with "reverence and awe" (Heb. 12:28) and with a "dignity" which is "fitting for sound doctrine" (Titus 2:1 NASB); because we are to "rejoice *with trembling*" (Ps. 2:11); because our mindset is to be consistent with physical acts of devotion such as bowing and kneeling. "O come let us worship and *bow down*," says the Psalmist, "Let us *kneel* before the Lord Our maker" (Ps. 96:6). Whether God is concerned with our posture in worship or not we'll leave to others to debate. However, all agree that He is concerned with our *attitude* in worship, and the attitude commanded is consistent with physical prostration: humility, reverence, and devotion. The Scottish theologian, Patrick Fairbairn (1805–1874), urges an "attitude of profound reverence and holy earnestness."[16] While cautioning against an artificial or sanctimonious manner, he

---

15 "The most logical place for the announcements ... is before the service begins," advises Rayburn in *O Come, Let Us Worship,* 170.

16 Patrick Fairbairn, *Pastoral Theology: A Treatise on the Office and Duties of the Christian Pastor* (1875; reprint, Audubon, New Jersey: Old Paths Publications, 1992), 314.

urges language "pervaded by a subdued, reverential, hallowed air."[17] All of the older authors urge ministers to spend much time on their knees prior to worship so that they will enter the pulpit in a proper frame of mind. "In the closet, alone with God, with the world shut out, is the proper place to get the mind and heart into the proper tone for conducting the public devotions," says nineteenth century American pastor Thomas Murphy (1823–1900).[18] The unction sought for the preaching should characterize "all the other parts of the service," as well.[19] The one leading worship should take care to avoid unduly drawing attention to himself. Do not attempt to "warm-up the crowd," like a stage performer, by being too cute, clever, or charming. Princeton Professor Samuel Miller (1769–1850) warns that "all coarseness, levity, or vulgarity – everything that borders on the ludicrous, or the want of real dignity, ought to be shunned …"[20] He speaks of the "gravity" of character and "solemn purpose" that ought to characterize his "every look, motion, and attitude in the pulpit."[21] Murphy asks, "What is more unbecoming than irreverence or levity in the presence of Jehovah?"[22]

Avoid, as we have said, even being too personal, too revealing. The worship service is not about the one leading. What he has just experienced or is now feeling is irrelevant. Lead the people to God, not to oneself. For this reason, standing behind the pulpit or lectern, or at least standing still, is to be preferred to wandering all over the platform or worse yet, up and down the aisles. We cannot point to chapter and verse to forbid this. However, we

---

17 Ibid., 313.

18 Thomas Murphy, *Pastoral Theology: The Pastor and the Various Duties of His Office* (1877; reprint, Audubon, New Jersey, Old Paths Publications, 1996), 214.

19 Ibid., 215.

20 Samuel Miller, *Clerical Manners and Habits: Addressed to a Student in the Theological Seminary at Princeton, N. J.* (Philadelphia: Presbyterian Board of Publications, 1852), 245.

21 Ibid., 251, 253.

22 Murphy, *Pastoral Theology,* 208.

can appeal to common sense. A wandering preacher does not get lost in the message. He does not become a little-noticed prop while God speaks to the people. No, too often he is the message. No minister should allow his movements, his abilities, his eloquence, his personality to become the prominent feature of the service. Maintain a God-centered tone and a God-centered focus throughout. The contemplation of God is to lead to joyful praise, and then to confession of sin, and then to a dependent looking to the means of grace, and finally, to a thankful response. Lead them, but quickly get out of the way and let the Holy Spirit, working through the Word, take over.

**Well-paced service**

Fifth, *establish a pace that is consistent with the urgency of the gospel.* It is difficult to pinpoint precisely what we mean by "pace." Yet we all know from experience of times when a service seemed to have been rushed, and of other times when it seemed to drag. Somewhere between these two extremes is a pace that is ideal. Though we cannot exactly identify what that pace is, or delineate principles by which to judge pace, we still know that finding the right pace is crucial if a congregation is to feel that a service is "alive," or that it "moves," or is "going somewhere." Is this not the terminology that is commonly used? Let us suggest the following.

For those who are inclined to race through a service of worship, remember that we are dealing with eternal things in worship. "Be not in haste to pass from one point of the service to another," cautions Miller.[23] Time for contemplation is needed if the people are to begin to "plumb the depths of the Almighty." When I first began my ministry in Savannah, an older member gently told me that I ought to shorten my sermon on communion Sunday because he felt the Lord's Supper was rushed. I promptly ignored his advice about my sermon (it was

---

23 Miller, *Clerical Manners*, 153.

already down to twenty-five minutes) but took very seriously the problem of a hurried communion service. We had to slow down. We cannot race if we are to observe the Supper properly. One may observe in evangelical circles a tendency both in preaching and in worship itself to mimic the rapidly changing images of television by darting from one thing to another. In preaching, this means short "sound bites" of text, story, illustration, a second story, exhortation, a third story, and finally back to the text. No time is left for thought. The pace won't allow it. It does allow for entertainment. Yet not for thought. We urge those who are speeding, slow down.

For those who are inclined to drag slowly through a service of worship, remember that we are dealing with eternal stakes in worship. Because we are worshiping the true God through the only Mediator, there is an urgency about all that we do. If what we believe is true, then there ought to be an urgency about our praying, singing, preaching, and even the transitions between each element. Every prayer pleads for grace. Every sermon urges souls to Christ. We have a finite amount of time. We have eternal truths to dispense. Consequently, the service ought to move briskly from one item to the next. It shouldn't be rushed. Yet it shouldn't drag either. The Rev. William Still (1911–97) wrote pointedly:

> What another profession calls 'timing' is very important if we are to gain and hold people's attention, to proclaim the greatest news on earth. Some men have no sense of split-second time which could make such a difference to their presentation of the truth … Be on your toes, and determine to hold the attention of your congregation from the first moment to the last. You have the greatest news in the world to tell them. Begin as if you knew that, and wanted them to know it.[24]

---

24 William Still, *Congregational Record and Bible Readings,* Gilcomston South Church of Scotland, Aberdeen, February 1989.

This dual sense of infinite truth and finite opportunities ought to result in an urgency which animates and enlivens our leadership in worship. We must make the most of each occasion. We must make the most of our time. Not even a moment may be wasted. Every second must be put to maximum use.

## Clergy-led services

Sixth, *the minister himself should lead the service.* Leave the leadership of worship in the hands of the ordained ministers. We confess to being uncomfortable with the growing practice of turning over the leadership of worship to "worship teams" made up of unordained musicians and others. Can this discomfort be justified as anything other than unwarranted clericalism? We think so. The restriction can be justified in precisely the same way in which regular preaching is restricted to those who have been examined both in theology and character and approved for licensure or ordination by presbytery. As we have seen, the thinking in the Reformed churches has been (whatever others have thought) that only those ought to preach who are theologically trained and examined, whose character has been observed and known to be of exceptional quality, and finally approved by the assembly of ministers and ruling elders. Only through the safeguard of licensure and ordination can the church be protected from the theological errors and ethical lapses of novices. The high privilege of public proclamation ought to be entrusted only to those who have been trained, examined, and approved at the highest levels. If this is true of those who do the public preaching in the Reformed churches, then who ought to do the public praying? Who ought to be selecting the hymns? It is only because we are no longer as careful as we once were to pray and sing biblical language and sound theology that we have forgotten the need of rigorous theological qualifications for those who lead in worship as well as those who preach. (So much error was spread in the early church through the hymns of heretics that the liturgy was purged of virtually all non-scriptural language around the fifth century. Hymns were not readmitted to the regular worship of the church until the twelfth century.)[25] We mention this not to advocate exclusive Psalm singing (though we do venerate the tradition), but to illustrate the point: leadership in worship ought to be left in the hands of those with thorough theological training and carefully assessed character. In other words, in the hands of ordained ministers.

If some are still unconvinced, we will provide an additional example, and an instructive one at that. Who may administer the sacraments in the Reformed churches? The consistent practice both among the continental Reformed and the English-speaking Reformed churches has been that *not even ruling elders may administer the sacraments.* The reason is simple. The warnings against abuse are so strong in Scripture (e.g. 1 Cor. 11:23-34), and the errors surrounding the sacraments that have plagued the church throughout its history are so serious that only biblically and theologically tested ministers may administer them. Even though ruling elders are examined theologically and for their character and spiritual maturity, they may not administer the sacraments because they have not been educated or examined at the level at which the ministers have. They are not qualified to explain the subtleties of our sacramental theology or to fence the table. What is true of preaching and the sacraments ought also be recognized of the other elements of worship and of the service as a whole.

For these reasons we urge that the minister take responsibility for the following:

---

25  J. G. Davies, *The New Westminster Dictionary of Liturgy and Worship*, (Philadelphia: The Westminster Press, 1986), article on "Hymns" by Mary Berry. She writes: The Roman Church did not admit (hymns) into the secular traffic until the twelfth century on account of the prejudice against importing other than biblical words into the liturgy, and even more because the form was used by heretics for propaganda purposes (262). See also Cheslyn Jones, Geoffrey Wainwright, eds., *The Study of Liturgy,* rev. ed. (New York: Oxford University Press, 1978, 1982), 509.

*1. The minister ought to plan the worship service.*
He should determine the order of service. He should determine which items to include and which to exclude. He should determine which of six prayers to use (invocation, confession, thanksgiving, intercession, illumination, benediction), and how to distribute them (singularly or in combination). He should explain the transitions between the items in the service. He should determine which hymns to use.

*2. The minister himself ought to control the worship service.*
He ought to for all the reasons stated above. In addition, given all the variables in the typical worship service and the constraints of time, he should be the one who makes the spontaneous adjustments, cutting and deleting, to keep the service on schedule. How often do sermons get crowded out because the various worship leaders are pursuing their own agendas without an eye to the whole? The minister must keep his reins on the whole service.

**Simple yet excellent services**
Seventh and last, *keep it simple yet excellent.* We repeatedly made this point in *Leading in Worship.*[26] Hughes Old has been a champion of simplicity in all of his writings. A particularly clear statement of it is made in his work on the liturgical use of the Psalms. Speaking of the processional Psalms he writes,

> It is doubtful if the New Testament Church ever used these psalms as processional psalms any more than the synagogue did. This kind of Temple ritual the synagogue showed little interest in trying to reproduce. Processions, entrance rites, as well as incense, vestments, musical instruments and the whole elaborate sacrificial system, were never received into the

---

26 Johnson, *Leading in Worship,* 122.

liturgical usage of the synagogue. In this the church followed the lead of the synagogue.[27]

We have no interest in elaborate rituals or ceremonies. Our worship is essentially spiritual and, as a consequence, simple. Jesus taught this when, in that most radical of statements in the New Testament, He declared that right worship is not that which is offered in Jerusalem or Samaria but that which is in spirit and truth (John 4:20-24). If it is no longer necessary to worship God in Jerusalem, then in one stroke the whole Old Testament system of worship comes tumbling down. Jerusalem was important only because it contained the temple. In the temple were found the altars, the sacrifices, the incense, the lambs, and so on (Heb. 9:2-5). Jesus swept it all away.[28] Our worship does not depend on holy buildings, holy hardware, rituals of approach, and holy days. It is all gone. Our worship is spiritual and simple. We ought to keep it such, with simple services of prayer, singing, preaching, and the sacraments. Don't turn the service into an elaborate musical production. Don't let it resemble a performance by professionals. We simply read the Word, preach the Word, sing the Word, pray the Word, and display the Word in the sacraments without extraneous words, movements, or gestures.[29] However, because it is simple, we have to work at it, both to keep it simple and to do it well. Worship "deserves special attention from the clergy of a simple ritual," says Shedd.[30]

---

27  Old, "Psalms as Christian Prayer," 112, 113.

28  We have established this point at length in *Reformed Worship*.

29  This formula of the Word read, preached, sung, prayed, and seen (or displayed) is elaborated on in *Reformed Worship*, 44-50, and provides the entire structure for both *Worshipping With Calvin* and *Serving With Calvin*.

30  Shedd, *Homiletics,* 275.

# 2

# Leading in Praise

Theological and moral relativism will never get out of the batter's box in the conservative Reformed churches. Ironically, aesthetic relativism is already rounding second base, and is well on its way to home. We say ironically because, ultimately, truth, righteousness, and beauty are interrelated. Indeed, they are perfectly integrated in God Himself. Beauty is ultimately a reflection of beauty as it is in God. The more one knows about the true God, the more one will know about true beauty. Both truth and righteousness have an aesthetic quality to them. When the truth is clearly articulated, when its coherence is demonstrated, its implications elaborated, it is lovely to see. Righteousness lived out in the lives of the saints, its order, its harmony, its innocence, and its purity, is likewise beautiful to behold. Ultimately, we cannot separate truth, righteousness, and beauty.

Moreover, in all three cases, we are able to understand and identify what they are. We know what truth, righteousness, and beauty are, though we know them with varying degrees of clarity. The Apostle Paul can urge us to "let [our] mind[s] dwell on" whatever things that are "true," "pure," and "lovely" (Phil. 4:8). What are these but the categories of truth, righteousness, and beauty? He assumes that we can identify such things and concentrate our minds on them. Perhaps in ways similar to the Law of God, the "beauty of God" is written on the hearts even of unbelievers, leaving them without excuse when they prefer the vulgar, the crude, and the ugly.[1]

Since this is so, we urge pastors to use the very finest suitable prose, poetry, and music in the worship of God. Do not settle for the blemished lambs of street language, cheap lyrics, and frothy music. We somehow have come to the place where many think that meaningful communication can only occur as the church adopts the idiosyncratic language and music of various subcultures, as though, for example, proper English cannot be understood and traditional hymns cannot be appreciated by anyone but old white people. One can envision the day when liturgies are prepared in the idioms of the biker, surfer, ghetto, teenage, barrio, and country-western subcultures, with music to match.[2] Where this all ends no one knows. Yet the momentum is building toward the twenty-first century version of the church of "me and thee ... and I'm not sure about thee." Rather than unifying the church, alleged requirements of "intelligibility" are dividing and potentially atomizing the church. After all, if I can only "relate" to *my* preferred forms of language and music, and if I otherwise am turned off by *your* preferred form, then I *must* have *my* own worship service, and *you* must have *yours*.

Better, it would seem, to use the highest common denominator and seek to draw the diversity of subcultures together on the basis of excellent but accessible English and music.[3] Among the greatest gifts of God to the church in the twentieth century is our rich heritage in language and song.

---

1 Kenneth A. Myers, *All God's Children and Blue Suede Shoes* (Westchester, Il: Crossway Books, 1989), 75-87, 119-132.

2 The arrival of cowboy churches confirms this trend. On ethnic churches in relation to Christian unity see Johnson, *Worshipping with Calvin,* 285-295.

3 On the importance of catholicity in worship see *Worshipping With Calvin,* 248-296.

We will now focus our attention on the church's songs.[4] The revolution in church song at the time of the Reformation was specifically a revival of congregational singing. The singing of the whole congregation, not a part of the congregation, not of a specialized choir, and not of solo performers is what we wish to encourage. To that end, we wish to encourage the use of the finest music and lyrics that the Christian church has been able to develop.

Many of history's greatest composers and songwriters were Christians. Bach, Handel, Beethoven, Mozart, and Brahms, as well as Lowell Mason and many others have left a treasure of music for the church, music that has stood the test of time. The church fathers, the monastic orders, the Reformers, the evangelical hymn writers of the eighteenth century (Watts, Wesley, Toplady, Newton, Cowper, Dodderidge, etc.), as well as some more modern writers have provided theologically rich and aesthetically outstanding lyrics for the church's praise. When choosing hymns, do not compromise quality for the shifting sands of popularity. Given that a worship service has a finite amount of time, one cannot justify using anything but the best that the church has to offer.

The objection that typically is raised is, who is to determine what is "best?" What is best for you may not be what is best for me. However, this argument assumes what we have already denied. Beauty is not relative. It is not merely in the eye of the beholder. Though we hesitate to identify the principles by which we distinguish "good" from "bad" music and lyrics, the discipline of aesthetic criticism has been around for a long time, dating back to the Ancient Greeks. For the Christian, beautiful music reflects the nature of God.

---

4  For historical and theological background on hymnody/psalmody, see *Worshipping With Calvin*, 222-248.

We recommend the following criteria for guiding song selection, for choosing songs that are *both* aesthetically rich *and* biblically sound.[5]

First, *is a given hymn singable?* Is the tune simple enough for a congregation to learn after working at it for a relatively short period of time? Notice we don't say that it must be so simple that it can be learned the first time through. Yet neither should it be so complex or difficult (not always the same thing) that the congregation is still stumbling the tenth time through it.[6] In this respect a significant number of contemporary tunes on the one hand, as well as classical-era tunes on the other, fail the test. Some of the popular Scripture songs are lovely when sung by solo performers, but because of irregular rhythms are utterly unsingable by congregations. There are classical tunes that must be classified as outstanding musically, but require trained choirs to be properly sung. The Reformation rightly restored *congregational* singing to the life of the church, replacing specialized choirs and vocalists. The first test of any hymn must be, can a congregation sing it?

Second, *is it biblically and theologically sound?* Truth is paramount. The church learns much of its theology through its songs, as Luther noted (lamented?) long ago. It also learns the language of Christian experience through what it sings. Instinctively, we turn to our songs both in time of crisis and great joy to find adequate language to express our response. Mary at the annunciation drew upon the song of Hannah (Luke 1:46-55; cf. 1 Sam. 2:1-10); Solomon at the dedication of the temple incorporated Psalm 132:8, 9 into his prayer (2 Chron. 6:40-42); Jesus on the cross used the words of

---

5 On the relationship between the tradition and the hymnal, see *Worshipping With Calvin* 281-285.

6 "The singing ought to be free from the faults which make it intolerable to persons of cultivated musical tastes, but it ought not to be of a kind in which only persons of cultivated musical taste can join," R. W. Dale, *Nine Lectures on Preaching,* 273.

Psalms 22:1 and 31:5 to express both His grief and hope (Matt. 27:46; Luke 23:46); and the early church responded to persecution with the language of Psalms 146 and 2 (Acts 4:24-30). In each case, the church's songs were interpreting experience and providing the language with which to express a faithful response. It is vital that our songs be theologically accurate.

Third, *is it biblically and theologically mature?* The Apostle Paul rebukes the Corinthians (1 Cor. 3:1ff) and the writer to the Hebrews scolds his readers for their failure to move on from "milk" to "solid food," for needing reinstruction regarding "elementary principles of the oracles of God," for failing to "press on to maturity" (Heb. 5:11-6:2 NASB). There is perhaps a place for children's choruses and campfire songs. However, that place is the Sunday School and summer camp, not the public worship services of the church. This is particularly true for churches in the Reformed tradition. Reformed churches are blessed with a great and sophisticated theology. However, it can only be sustained if it is constantly being reinforced in our public worship. Realize the obvious – our doctrines and practices are communicated and learned in our primary congregational gatherings or they are not being communicated and learned in any significant sense at all. Yes, there may be some who are picking up the Reformed faith through blogs and podcasts, through their own private reading or through small, specialized study groups. Yet, for the bulk of the congregation, Reformed, that is, biblical, doctrine will remain foreign. Consequently, our sermons certainly, but also our administration of the sacraments, our prayers and our songs must reinforce our distinctive teachings, or those distinctive teachings will slowly evaporate from popular consciousness. Not just our preaching but our prayers and songs and sacraments must express the conviction that God is sovereign, that salvation is by Christ alone, faith alone, and by grace alone, that Christ is spiritually present in the sacrament, and so on. All of this is to say that it is crucial that the church's songs be substantial enough to express accurately mature Christian belief as well as the subtlety of Christian experience.

For these reasons, we have a decided preference for metrical Psalms and time-proven hymns, particularly those of the eighteenth century, the "golden age" of hymn writing. Simplistic, sentimental, repetitious songs by their very nature cannot carry the weight of Reformed doctrine and will leave the people of God ill-equipped on occasions of great moment. The problem with them, and with late-nineteenth century gospel songs as well, is not when they were written, as though there were something inherently wrong with anything modern, but their form and consequent content. Their form cannot accommodate serious thought. The Reformed faith, by way of contrast, cannot survive the absence of serious thought.

Let's imagine an occasion of great grief. The heart yearns for language with which to express that grief. What can the contemporary Christian music world supply? One might be able to name a couple of titles. Yet wouldn't one have to admit that, for the most part, the popular choruses are too simplistic, too light, too superficial to handle the occasion? Those whose churches feed them a steady diet of choruses and gospel songs lack the resources to understand and express their hearts. These songs are by and large "happy songs," which is all they are meant to be. However, those whose churches feed their people a steady diet of metrical Psalms and time-proven hymns might respond by singing any of the following:

Psalm 23 – "The Lord's my shepherd, I'll not want"
Psalm 46 – "God is our refuge and our strength"
Psalm 91 – "Who with God most high finds shelter"
"Abide with me, fast falls the even tide"
"Be still my soul, the Lord is on thy side"

"When peace like a river attendeth my way"
"Whate'er my God ordains is right"

Dr. Douglas Kelly tells of an oft-repeated scene in eighteenth-
and nineteenth-century Scotland, of families split by the massive
migrations to North America waving good-bye to each other, as
both those on the docks and those on the ships launching out to
sea sang the stirring Twenty-Third Psalm, concluding,

> Goodness and mercy all my life shall surely follow me;
> And in God's house for evermore my dwelling-place shall be.

One might perhaps be able to justify singing the simple choruses
as a temporary measure, designed to acclimate new believers to
singing before moving on to songs more substantial. A limited
use of such targeting the aptitude of the young and immature,
aiming in doing so to eventually move them up to more serious
songs, is understandable. However, the priority should always be
the canonical Psalms and theologically rich hymns.

Fourth, *is it emotionally balanced?* This is perhaps the most
subjective point of the very subjective topic of human preferences.
Yet there is a suitable balance between the emotive content and
the truth content of our songs, and our prayers and sermons for
that matter. Strong emotional appeal without strong biblical-
theological expression is manipulation, not worship. Churches
are employing the tricks of the propagandist, not the truths of
the prophets, when they use syrupy songs devoid of theological
content. Tunes ought not to overwhelm the words. Years ago,
John Stott (1921–2011) told a gathering of theological students
in England that he would never allow the chorus "Alleluia," be
sung in his church for that reason. The people were moved when
they sang it, the congregation might be visibly *swaying*, but what
were they *saying*? Almost nothing. They were singing a blank
check, with each one filling in his own content. When repetition

comes to this, lyrics bear more of a resemblance to eastern mantras than to Christian praise. Indeed, while vacationing a few years back, I simultaneously viewed on a broadcast a "praise gathering" of Botswami somebody in Oregon and on another station what I regarded as an extremely charismatic praise service. As I flipped from one to the other, it was difficult to see any difference. Both groups raised their hands. Both closed their eyes. Both repeated their peculiar sounds over and over again. Both swayed, or trembled as they did so. Are we not to love God with our minds? Are not the songs with which we sing and make melody in our hearts also supposed to teach and admonish (Eph. 5:19; Col. 3:16)? Are we not to sing with the spirit and "with the mind also?" (1 Cor. 14:15). Are our songs and prayers not meant to edify (1 Cor. 14:17-18)? What God has joined together ought not to be broken asunder.

On the other hand, the words ought not to overwhelm the tune either. Rich theological and biblical content joined to a lousy tune is undesirable as well. What we are looking for is balance. We find this balance of words and tunes which carry the words in such classic hymns as "Joy to the World," "Hark the Herald Angel Sings," "Holy, Holy, Holy," "Praise to the Lord the Almighty," "Crown Him with Many Crowns," "When I Survey the Wondrous Cross," "Here O My Lord I See Thee Face to Face," "How Sweet and Awful Is the Place." The music in each case underscores the content of the words.

Fifth, *is it demographically comprehensive?* Our songs should not target one demographic at the expense of the others. The instrumentation (if any) should not privilege one generation over the rest. Ideally, the songs selected will be recognizably those of the church, small "c" catholic church. They will not belong to any single group in the church and so will belong to all the groups in the church. This is the great advantage of singing out of the hymnal and psalter. They represent the best lyrics and music developed by the church over centuries. They have stood the test of time. At the same time, there is room for the addition of new songs to the music "canon" as they gain acceptance throughout the church.

Some ministers make the mistake of turning over this last responsibility to the music director or musician.[7] Our question is, why? Is he better trained theologically to do so? Does he have greater knowledge of the content of the weekly sermon and what would better tie in with it? Is he more aware of the need and knowledge of the congregation? We trust that the answer to these questions would be no. The only reasonable justification might be the obvious one: that he knows the hymnal better than the minister. This points out a larger problem. Many of the younger ministers serving Reformed churches today are men who were converted in high school or college through campus ministries. Their formative spiritual experiences occurred in the context of those organizations. Many of these men went directly from college to seminary, and from there into the churches. Consequently, they bring with them a vast ignorance of the church, its life, and its devotional forms.

I can think of a fine minister for whom the above description fits, who never attended Sunday night services, and when he became a solo pastor, had no interest in having a Sunday night service. He had no background and consequently no understanding of the ways in which Sunday night services function in the life of a congregation. The same is true for the order of service and hymnody. Many are pastoring churches who have never participated in a traditional Reformed service. Many are ignorant of the rich treasury of hymns that is the heritage of the church. I console myself in thinking that worship services

---

7 "The choice of hymns will, of course, be absolutely in your own hands," R. W. Dale, *Nine Lectures on Preaching* (London: Hodder and Stoughton, nd), 277.

sometimes look as they do because those leading them just don't know any better.

Let us then urge those who have or shall take pastoral charges to be careful students of the hymnal and psalter. W.G.T. Shedd (1820–1894), in *Homiletics and Pastoral Theology* (1867), devotes considerable space to hymn-selection, all the while urging the minister to study the hymnody of the church, and specifically the hymnbook of the church to which he ministers so that he will "obtain that taste and feeling for sacred lyric poetry which will guide him, as by a sure instinct, to the choice of the best and most appropriate hymns."[8] When I first began to lead worship services, I asked a pianist in the church to play for me every single selection in the hymnal. I rated the words and tunes of each on a scale of one to ten, recorded my ratings, and then created a list of the several hundred earning a score of seven or greater. On that list I mark the dates when hymns are used, color-coding the year for easy reference. The result has been a vast expansion of my knowledge of available and useful hymns. Both the new and old *Trinity Hymnal* are goldmines of devotional material. Study them. The late Robert G. Rayburn (1915–1990), in his very useful study, *O Come, Let Us Worship*, estimates that the average congregation uses about thirty or thirty-five songs or hymns in a year. We use over 200 different hymns and Psalms each year. This wider exposure enriches the worship of the church as well as the personal devotional life of the members of the congregation.

We have now completed our consideration of the aesthetics and content of the church's songs except to make this final observation. Evangelical Christians have long been accused of reducing all worship to the sermon. It is doubtful that this was ever a fair generalization. Today, evangelicals are devoting considerable thought to the whole service of worship. Yet nowhere are we still vulnerable to this charge more than in our

---

8 Shedd, *Homiletics,* 270.

lack of concern for the selection of our songs. Here we still seem to be saying, loudly and on key, that it doesn't matter what we sing; only the sermon matters.

# 3

# Leading in Prayer

Offering prayer in public is an aspect of leading in worship that deserves focused attention. Because the Lord's Day worship service is a *public* service, the prayers in those services are of necessity public and partake of the qualities of public ordinances. This means that public prayer will differ from private prayer in both its subject matter and its aim. Namely, public prayer must edify the public. Prayers offered in public are audible, not silent, and must be intelligible because they aim at not personal but public edification. Their purpose is to bless both God and the congregation. There are two audiences, one on earth and one in heaven. This is precisely the apostle Paul's point in 1 Corinthians 14:14-19 whether considering preaching, signing, or prayer. If one prays "in the Spirit" (whatever exactly that means) so that one cannot be understood, the prayer may be a sincere expression of thanksgiving, but (and here is the crucial point) "the other man is not edified." Better are five intelligible words that may "instruct others" than "ten thousand words in a tongue" (1 Cor. 14:17, 19 nasb). Public prayer, while addressed to God is for public edification and instruction. It is another kind of pulpit speech, closely related to preaching.

This understanding of public prayer was typical of early Protestantism and the whole subsequent free church tradition (Presbyterian, Congregational, Baptist, Methodist). Skill in praying publicly was considered a gift given by God to those whom He calls into the public ministry, and was to be cultivated through prayer disciplines and the careful study of the devotional language of the Bible. Because faith comes by hearing the Word of God, the use of scriptural language and allusions in prayer was understood to be of critical importance (Rom. 10:17). The congregation will be edified as Scripture-enriched, impassioned prayers are offered in public worship, they believed.

Convictions like these lie behind the liturgical reforms of Bucer, Farel, Calvin, and Knox, as they wrote Scripture-based prayers in their Orders of Worship and encouraged free prayers.[1] They are clearly evident in the attempted reforms of the English Puritans, as seen in their Middleburg Liturgy, in the Westminster Directory for the Public Worship of God, and in Richard Baxter's Savoy or Reformed Liturgy, presented to Charles II in Puritanism's final attempt to reform the Prayer Book. Throughout the Reformation and Second Reformation period of over one hundred years, the theme is the same: written prayers must be more scriptural and free prayers must be permitted so that the people may be edified as the church prays.[2] Pastoral concern drove these liturgical reforms.

Following the Acts of Uniformity and the "Great Ejection" of the Puritans from the Church of England in 1662, Anglicanism returned to a strictly "liturgical" worship, consisting of fixed forms and allowing no divergence from those forms. However, the dissenting churches continued to emphasize Scripture-enriched free prayers. For generations, ministers of the Scottish

---

1 Bard Thompson, *Liturgies of the Western Church* (Philadelphia: Fortress Press, 1961), 159-224, 287-307.

2 Ibid., 311-405.

Presbyterian, English non-conformists and their American sister churches learned to pray by consulting Matthew Henry's *A Method for Prayer* or Isaac Watt's *A Guide to Prayer*. The former of these, by the way, appeared in over thirty editions between 1710 and 1865.[3] Henry understood that the one who prays publicly must not only look within his own heart as he prays, but must seek "the edification also of those that join with him; and both in matter and words should have an eye to that."[4] He designed his book as a help for those who lead in prayer, organizing his work according to the standard categories of adoration, confession, thanksgiving, and intercession, as well as providing a few examples or forms of prayer for various occasions. He restricted himself almost entirely to the language of Scripture, the only exceptions being some section headings. He goes on in this fashion, Scripture phrase after Scripture phrase, for nearly two hundred and fifty pages! Remarkably, he says in his introduction (as he explains that much more could have been written), "I have only set down such *as first occurred to my thoughts.*"[5]

Henry wrote in 1710 and, according to Hughes Old, "for generations shaped the prayer life of Protestantism."[6] Writing only a few years later (1715), Isaac Watts stressed the same themes, and in 1849, Samuel Miller published his *Thoughts on Public Prayer*,[7] carrying these emphases forward to the beginning of the twentieth century. Public prayer, they all agreed, like public preaching, must edify the whole congregation, and to do so, it must be rich with scriptural language and allusions.

---

3  Hughes Oliphant Old, *Worship That is Reformed According to Scripture: Guides to the Reformed Tradition* (Atlanta: John Knox Press, 1984), 102.

4  Henry, *Method*, xii.

5  Ibid, xv, my emphasis.

6  Old, *Themes and Variations for a Christian Doxology* (Grand Rapids: Eerdmans, 1992), 12.

7  Samuel Miller, *Thoughts on Public Prayer* (1849; Harrisonburg, Virginia: Sprinkle Publications, 1985).

Given this perspective, it is not surprising to learn that most of the older manuals on preaching (e.g. Perkins, Doddridge, Dabney, Dale, Beecher, Broadus, Jowett)[8] included instruction on and urged the use of Scripture in public prayer. They perpetuated the prevailing Protestant understanding that preaching and prayer are parallel forms of edifying public speech even as William Perkins had labeled it "the second aspect of prophesying" years before.[9] For example, Henry Ward Beecher, delivering the first of the famous "Yale Lectures on Preaching" in 1872, entitled a section of his work "Prayer as an element of Preaching." Later Yale lecturers Brooks, Dale, and Jowett continued to reflect the same concerns. Similarly, most of the older manuals on pastoral theology (e.g. Fairbairn, Murphy, Porter, Shedd, Spurgeon)[10] included sections on public prayer, typically under the heading of "preaching" or "homiletics," urging all the same themes. A solid consensus on the nature and language and value of public prayer can be seen in the Reformed tradition.

## RECENT TIMES

Strange amnesia, however, seems to have set in early in the twentieth century. Few books since then have been written

---

8 William Perkins, *The Art of Prophesying* (1606; Edinburgh: The Banner of Truth Trust, 1996); Philip Doddridge, *Lectures on Preaching* (London: R. Edwards, 1807); Robert Dabney, *Sacred Rhetoric or Course of Lectures on Preaching* (1870; Edinburgh; The Banner of Truth Trust, 1979); R. W. Dale, *Nine Lectures on Preaching* (London: Hodder and Stoughton, n.d.); Henry Ward Beecher, *Yale Lectures on Preaching* (New York: Fords, Howard, and Hulbert, 1893); J. A. Broadus, *On the Preparation and Delivery of Sermons* Revised Edition (1870; Nashville: Broadman Press, 1944); J. H. Jowett, *The Preacher: His Life and Work* (New York: George H. Doran Company, 1912).

9 Perkins, *The Art of Prophesying,* 77.

10 Patrick Fairbairn, *Pastoral Theology: A Treatise on the Office and Duties of the Christian Pastor* (1875; Audubon, New Jersey: Old Paths Publications, 1992); Thomas Murphy, *Pastoral Theology: The Pastor and the Various Duties of His Office* (1877; Audubon, New Jersey: Old Paths Publications, 1996); Ebenezer Porter, *Lectures on Homiletics and Preaching, and on Public Prayer; Together with Sermons and Letters* (New York; Flagg, Gould and Newman, 1834); W.G.T. Shedd, *Homiletics and Pastoral Theology* (1867; The Banner of Truth Trust, 1965); C. H. Spurgeon, *An All-Around Ministry: Addresses to Ministers and Students* (1900; Edinburgh: The Banner of Truth Trust, 1965).

recently on the subject of public prayer, and few of the older manuals were republished for wide circulation until the mid-1980's when Miller, and then 1994 when Henry was republished by Reformed Academic Press.[11] Those few authors who did write on public prayer did so in a historical vacuum with respect to this free prayer tradition.

Whether examining books on pastoral theology or those on public worship or the evangelical and Reformed periodical literature, little was said for nearly a century about public prayer, its pastoral value, and even less about filling such prayers with scriptural content.[12]

If I may add my own anecdotal evidence, not once in my first forty years did anyone suggest to me that I ought to make use of Scripture in my public prayers. Not once did anyone suggest that there is a unique sanctifying power in public prayers enriched by scriptural language and allusions. Not once did anyone urge consideration of public prayer as an important means of grace paralleling preaching itself. The more general practice of praying Scripture was never mentioned through years of Sunday school and church attendance in my childhood and youth. It was not mentioned during four years of college parachurch Bible studies, camps and conferences. It was not mentioned during four years of seminary. It was not mentioned during the first fifteen years of post-seminary ministry.

Given the scant attention that public prayer received in the twentieth century, one may safely conclude that little vision for its pastoral value remained at the dawn of the twenty-first century. Yet prayer, like preaching, is a means of grace, as any child brought up on the *Shorter Catechism* knows (Q. 88). This

---

11 An edited version of Watts' *Guide to Prayer* was published on a limited basis in 1948 by Epworth Press in Great Britain.

12 For the data behind these claims, see the original *Westminster Theological Journal* articles mentioned in the preface.

is true not just of private prayers, but public as well. Troubled souls at times need not counsel, even nouthetic (i.e. Bible-based) counseling, but passionate and biblical prayer. A pastor's scripturally-enriched public prayers may soothe the troubled, calm the anxious, answer the doubting, stiffen the wavering, break the unrepentant, and in so doing, remove the need of further counseling or preaching. Few have understood the role of public prayer as a means of grace. Too often, public prayer has been seen as a burden to bear, not a blessing to receive.

The lone exception in this disappointing survey of declension has been Hughes Oliphant Old (1933–2016), who, for over two decades, was something of a voice crying in the wilderness. Following his seminal study *The Patristic Roots of Reformed Worship*,[13] he has three times published works calling for a renewed study of Matthew Henry and a return to Scripture-based prayer[14] beginning with his *Worship: That is Reformed According to Scripture,* first published in 1985. A decade later, he published *Leading in Prayer* (1995) which purports to be a Henry or Watts for the twenty-first century. "I publish this book" he says, "much in the same spirit as Matthew Henry published his *Method of Prayer* or Isaac Watts published a similar sort of volume a generation later."[15] Prayer, he says, has "its own language, its own vocabulary, and its own imagery. This language is not simply a matter of style. Prayer, particularly Christian prayer, *uses biblical language*."[16] A revival of the historic Protestant practice of Scripture-enriched prayer stands at or near the top of the reforms that are crucial to the health of the church today.

---

13  Hughes Oliphant Old, *The Patristic Roots of Reformed Worship* (Zurich: Theologischer Verlag, 1970).

14  Old, *Worship*; idem, *Themes and Variations*; idem, *Leading in Prayer* (Grand Rapids: Eerdmans, 1995).

15  Old, *Leading in Prayer*, 3.

16  Ibid., 7, my emphasis.

## PERSONAL EXPERIENCE

Given the lack of instruction mentioned above, my own pilgrimage to these convictions has been slow, accidental (in a Calvinistic sense) and, at times, painful. Yet I am sure that my experience parallels that of many others as well, who, upon reflection, may recall similar incidences.

My first serious thoughts about public prayers began dramatically in the spring of 1978, as an intern at the St. David's Broomhouse Church of Scotland, in Edinburgh. Rev. C. Peter White, the minister, was ill one Sunday, leaving me to lead the services and preach. It was the practice of the leadership of the congregation to gather thirty minutes or so before the beginning of worship and pray for the services of the day. A group of about fifteen took their seats in a large circle in a private room. When it looked like all who were coming were present, they rose up turned and faced their chairs, knelt down on their knees, and began to pray. Though this was a working-class congregation, and though none of those present were college educated, and even a few were functionally illiterate, I soon realized that I was in way over my head.

I came to Scotland from Southern California via Trinity College, Bristol, England, arriving full of hope that I might be the means of ushering in renewal in Scotland. After all, I knew the essential principles of small-group discipleship and was armed with all the latest choruses and "Scripture-songs." As these Scots began to pray, I realized that something was seriously amiss. I had never heard such prayers. They were full of God, full of Scripture, full of passion, full of reverence, and full of humility. My prayers, by comparison, had always been of the "just really" variety – trite, self-centered, too casual, and too familiar. The spiritual maturity of their prayers exposed my spiritual poverty. The God that they knew was almost a different God. That short experience had a devastating impact on me. I could just barely persuade myself to go on and lead the service. I had no business leading these people in worship. They should be leading me. I returned to Trinity College humbled, seriously questioning my call, unsettled for another six months. That summer I returned to what was then my home church, the Lake Avenue Congregational Church in Pasadena, California, a church in which I had served as a summer intern, and refused to be involved in any leadership in ministry. I needed to sit quietly and learn, I told my supervisors.

The next year back in Bristol, I began to attend the Buckingham Baptist Church pastored by the Rev. Ron Clark. He was preaching on Psalm 23. Week by week, his sermons were profoundly moving, using Scripture in a way that gave his preaching a unique unction. Equally moving were his prayers. I was not consciously aware of why they were so moving, but looking back later I came to recognize – they were full of the language and allusions of Scripture.

Several years later, a friend loaned me a tape of a Lloyd-Jones sermon on evangelism. The first half of the sermon he attacked the Arminians for unbiblical preaching. As all the Calvinists were saying "amen," he turned his considerable artillery on them with devastating effect. I was at the time constructing a fence in a friend's backyard. I had to stop to dry my eyes. Never had I heard such preaching. Then he began to pray. I can still recall a few of the phrases: "in wrath remember mercy;" "turn us and we shall be turned;" "revive Thy work in the midst of the years." Full of lament and passion, he prayed on. It was overwhelming. I was utterly undone by the extraordinary power of that concluding prayer.

Years later at Independent Presbyterian Church, I began to notice that several of the laymen who gathered weekly for our Tuesday morning prayer meeting prayed with particular unction, and made, not coincidentally, pointed use of Scripture as they prayed. One man in particular arrested my attention as he prayed, "Lord, our Lord, how majestic is your name *in all the earth!*" (Ps 8:1).

The conviction that one ought to use Scripture in prayer grew through the years. The clincher came in the mid-1990's when I began to read Matthew Henry's *A Method for Prayer*.

Over a fifteen-year period, I slowly came to realize the importance of prayer, and particularly of using the language of Scripture in prayer. Those coming out of a "low" or "non-liturgical" church tradition are often amazed at the amount of Scripture found in the traditional liturgies, far more than in the average evangelical church. We've noted one reason for this – the church of late antiquity responded to various heretics by banishing from her liturgy all non-scriptural language, especially hymns, which the heretics (such as Arius) were especially skilled at composing. Still today, the liturgies of the Lutheran, Anglican, Orthodox, and Roman churches reflect this scriptural emphasis. Previous generations of Presbyterians and Baptists didn't find this emphasis so remarkable because their "free" worship, with metrical Psalms, Scripture-based prayers, Bible reading and biblical preaching, was equally rife with the language of Scripture. Yet today, even those churches which are not on the "Durham Trail," as D.G. Hart calls it, that is, the churches that are not deconstructing traditional worship in order to appeal to tastes shaped by today's popular culture, retain very little of Scripture in their services.[17] Not much is read. Sermons are more topical than expository. Fragments, at best, are sung. As for the prayers, "One has to admit," says Hughes Old, "that the spontaneous prayer one often hears in public worship is an embarrassment to the tradition."[18]

---

17 Originally entitled, "Evangelicals on the Durham Trail," it appeared as "Post-Modern Evangelical Worship," *Calvin Theological Journal* 30 (1995) 451-59.

18 Old, *Leading in Prayer*, 5.

## RECOMMENDATIONS FOR PUBLIC PRAYER

We have several recommendations for the improvement of public prayer in light of what we have discussed so far. Thankfully the twenty-first century has seen the republication of Henry and Watts as well as C. H. Spurgeon's *The Pastor in Prayer,*[19] and O. Palmer Robertson's reworking and updating of Henry's *A Method for Prayer* entitled *A Way to Pray.*[20]

### Scriptural prayers

First, *public prayers should utilize the language of Scripture.* Obviously, this is our primary point. Listen to the voices from the past as they universally urge this practice. Matthew Henry says, "I would advise that the *sacred* dialect be most used, and made familiar to us and others in our dealing about *sacred* things; that language Christian people are most accustomed to, most affected with, and will most readily agree to."[21] Scottish minister and theologian Patrick Fairbairn (1805–1874) urges that the whole prayer "should be cast much in the mould of Scripture, and should be marked by a free use of its language."[22] R.L. Dabney says, "Above all should the minister enrich his prayers with the language of Scripture."[23] The Reformed past is unanimous in this conviction. Consider the following.

*1. This is the pattern found in Scripture itself.*
The importance of Scripture-based prayer is not merely the opinion of the Reformers or of eighteenth- and nineteenth-

---

19 C. H. Spurgeon, *The Pastor in Prayer* (1893; Edinburgh: The Banner of Truth Trust, 2004).

20 O. Palmer Robertson, *A Way to Pray* (Edinburgh: The Banner of Truth Trust, 2010).

21 Henry, *Method,* xiv.

22 Fairburn, *Pastoral Theology*, 317.

23 Dabney, *Sacred Rhetoric*, 358; see also Miller, *Thoughts*, 217; Murphy, *Pastoral Theology*, 213; Broadus, *Preparation and Delivery*, 368-69.

century evangelical theologians. It is also the pattern that we see in Scripture. The biblical saints learned God-pleasing devotional language from the Bible. They often used the language and themes of Scripture to interpret and express their experience. Consider for instance Moses' seminal revelatory experience in Exodus 34:6-7 (NASB).

> Then the Lord passed by in front of him and proclaimed, "The Lord, the Lord God, compassionate and gracious, slow to anger, and abounding in lovingkindness and truth; who keeps lovingkindness for thousands, who forgives iniquity, transgression and sin; yet He will by no means leave the guilty unpunished, visiting the iniquity of fathers on the children and on the grandchildren to the third and fourth generations."

The echo of this revelation is heard on at least thirteen additional occasions in the Old Testament as later prophets learned from Moses how to praise God.[24] Where then are we to learn the language of Christian devotion if not from Scripture? That this is less than self-evident to a tradition whose defining principle has been that worship must be regulated by God's Word is surprising indeed.[25] Since our minds are "factories for idols," to borrow Calvin's phrase, we must be taught the language of prayer. Isn't that the point of the disciples' request of Jesus, "Lord, teach us to pray" (Luke 11:1)? Doesn't the Apostle Paul acknowledge that "we do not know what to pray for as we ought?" (Rom 8:26). Isn't that indeed the point of the book of Psalms? Were the Psalms not provided to teach the people of God the language of devotion with which God is pleased? If Jesus in the supreme crisis of His life drew upon the Psalter in order to understand and express His devotion and experience (Ps. 22:1; 31:5), then we can do no less.

---

24  E.g. Numbers 14:18; 2 Chronicles 30:9; Nehemiah 9:17,31; Psalm 103:8; 111:4; 112:4; 116:5; 145:9; Joel 2:13; Jonah 4:2; etc.

25  On the regulative principle see *Reformed Worship*, 33-44.

*2. There is a special efficacy in Scripture-based prayer.*

No prayers more accurately reflect the will of God than those which use the language which God Himself puts into our mouths. No request is more sure to be granted than that which expresses what God Himself has promised to fulfill. No petition is more sure to be answered than that which pleads for that which God requires. Pray the promises and commands of Scripture. This principle is evident in James 1. Does God command that we be wise? Of course He does. It follows then that we should ask for it. "If any of you lacks wisdom, let him ask God, who gives generously to all without reproach, and it will be given him" (James 1:5). Similarly, pray the promise of 1 John 1:9, that if we confess our sins God is faithful and just to forgive our sins and cleanse us of all unrighteousness. Claim the promise of John 3:16 in prayer, that "whosoever believeth in him should not perish (KJV)." Plead that the people of God will be holy even as God is holy (1 Pet. 1:16). Plead that they will love one another and bear one another's burdens (Gal. 6:2). Faith comes by hearing the word of God doesn't it (Rom. 10:17)? The word prayed in the hearing of the congregation will be efficacious to the salvation of their souls.

*3. There is a special comfort in scriptural prayer.*

It is one thing to pray, "Lord, please be with us through this day." It is quite another to pray, "Lord remember your promise, 'I will never leave nor forsake you'" (Heb. 13:5). Can we not sense the difference? It is one thing to pray, "As we begin our prayer, we thank you for the privilege of bringing our petitions to you." It is quite another to pray, "We come at Your invitation, O Christ, for you have promised, 'Ask, and it will be given to you; seek, and you will find; knock, and it will be opened to you.' And so we come asking, seeking, and knocking" (Matt. 7:7-8). It is one thing to pray in the midst of tragedy, "Lord we know that you have a plan." That is a true, valid, and comforting thing to pray. Even so, it is quite another to pray, "O Lord, you have numbered the hairs upon our heads. You are working all things after the counsel of your will. Not even a sparrow may fall from a tree apart from you. You cause all things to work together for good for those who love you, and are called according to your purpose" (Matt. 10:29-30; Eph. 1:11; Rom. 8:28). Ministers may more effectively comfort the hearts of their people by echoing the promises of Scripture in their prayers.

### 4. Scriptural prayer reinforces the ministry of the Word.

As noted above, one reason why previous generations of evangelicals were more biblically literate than ours is that there was more Bible content in their services than in ours. The Word preached and the Word prayed and the Word sung were constantly reinforcing each other. The Romantic movement of the late nineteenth and early twentieth centuries removed much of the biblical and theological content of our hymns. Only fragments of scriptural expression remain in our songs. We've already commented on the state of preaching and praying. The irony that the churches that profess to believe in the inerrancy of Scripture make such little use of Scripture and are becoming increasingly ignorant of Scripture is bitter indeed. What a difference it will make if our ministers will call the people to worship with Scripture, invoke the presence of God with scriptural praise, sing a metrical Psalm, confess sin using Scripture language, read the Scripture, preach an expository sermon, sing a scriptural hymn, build their intercessions around the five-fold categories found in Scripture, used by the early church, and revived by the Reformers, and conclude with a scriptural benediction.[26] This done, Sunday morning and evening, fifty-two weeks a year, year after year will build a strong church, one characterized by scriptural literacy

---

26 See Johnson, *Leading in Worship*, 10n.15, 34n.4, and 52-54.

and spiritual maturity. If a church will worship in this way, its growth may be slower than is acceptable to many. It may require that one take a longer view than is customary today. One may not gather large crowds overnight. However, in the long run a church that builds the foundation of the words of Christ will endure like a rock and not be shaken.

***

Given the above, it is vital that ministers study the prayers and devotional language of Scripture. There is much to learn from the prayers of praise of David in 1 Chronicles 29 or the composite prayer of Paul in 1 Timothy (1 Tim. 1:17; 6:15-16).

There is much to learn from the prayers of confession of David (Ps. 51) and Daniel (Dan. 9). Psalm 43:4 and Ephesians 3:18-19 supply language for prayers of illumination.

> O send out Thy light and Thy truth, let them lead me; let them bring me to Thy holy hill, and to Thy dwelling places. (Ps. 43:3 NASB)

> May (we) be able to comprehend with all the saints what is the breadth and height and depth, and to know the love of Christ which surpasses knowledge, that (we) may be filled up to all the fulness of God. (Eph. 3:18-19 NASB)

There is much to learn from the prayers of intercession of the apostle Paul for the saints in Ephesus, Philippi, and Colossae (Eph. 1:15-23; Phil. 1:9-11; Col. 1:9-11). Study the prayers of the Bible.[27]

---

27 Eg. Genesis 18:23-33 (intercession); Exodus 15:1-18 (praise); 32:11-14 and 33:12-17 (intercession); Numbers 11:10-15 (complaint); 14:11-19 (pleading); 1 Samuel 2:1-10 (praise); II Samuel 7:18-29 (thanksgiving); I Chronicles 29:11-20 (praise); I Kings 3:6-9 (for wisdom); 8:22-53; 54-61 (praise); II Chronicles 6:14-42 (praise and petition); II Kings 19:14-19 (intercession); Jeremiah 32:16-25 (praise and questioning); Ezra 9:5-

In addition, study the phrasing, vocabulary, and broader context of Scripture. Don't just open the worship service by praying whatever pops into your head. Pray, "O Lord we have come to worship and bow down, to kneel before You the Lord our Maker; for You are our God, and we are the people of Your pasture, the sheep of Your hand" (Ps. 95). Don't just pray, "Lord save our covenant children." Pray instead, "Lord remember your promise to be a God to us and to our children, and so save our covenant children." Pray back to God His promises. Pray back to God His ideals as found in the Beatitudes (Matt. 5) and the fruit of the Spirit (Gal. 5). Pray back to God His revelation of His own nature. Pray back to God those things that He requires of us in His Word. For example, why not turn Ephesians 5:1-17 into a prayer:

> that we might be imitators of God, as beloved children, and walk in love, just as Christ also loved us," and "that immorality, and impurity, and greed might not be named among us.

Find key phrases and precious promises and turn them into prayer. There is almost no limit to what can be done. Even historical allusions can be profitably employed in prayer. Samuel Miller provides several examples that are worthy of study.[28]

Especially helpful in the study of prayer in addition to the older volumes already cited are a number of studies of personal prayer such as Richard L. Pratt's *Pray With Your Eyes Open*,[29] W.

---

15 (confession); Nehemiah 9:5-27 (praise and petition); Daniel 9:1-19 (confession and petition); Habakkuk 1:12-17 (questioning); Luke 1:46-55 (praise); Luke 1:68-79 (praise); Luke 2:29-32 (praise); Acts 4:24-30 (praise and petition); Colossians 1:9-12; Ephesians 1:1-23; Philippians 1:9-11 (praise and petition); Revelation 4:8-5:14 (praise).

28 Eg. Miller, *Public Prayer*, 277-278.

29 Richard L. Pratt, *Pray with Your Eyes Open* (Phillipsburg, N.J.: Presbyterian and Reformed Pub. Co., 1987).

Graham Scroggie's *Paul's Prison Prayers*,[30] Donald Cogan's *The Prayers of the New Testament*,[31] and Herbert Lockyer's *All the Prayers of the Bible*.[32] Better yet, get a copy of Henry's *A Method for Prayer* and read it over and over again.

## Planned

Second, public prayers should be *planned*. This is obviously necessary if the preceding point is to be realized, if one is to be able to pray in the language of the Bible. Yet planning is necessary for other reasons as well. It is sad to hear the careless language, the imprecision, and the incoherence of many pulpit prayers today. I suspect, though I cannot prove, that many ministers give no thought whatsoever to what they intend to pray beforehand. Willimon complains that "many of our pastoral prayers are a maze of poorly thought out, confusing clichés, hackneyed expressions, shallow constructions, and formalized, impersonal ramblings."[33] All of the old commentators are of one mind on the need of planning public prayers. One ought no more pray without preparation than preach. Fairbairn says, "I would earnestly advise a certain measure of special preparation for the devotional work of the sanctuary."[34] He encourages the use of an outline, and even the practice of writing out one's prayers, not in order to read them, but in order to organize one's thoughts. W.G.T. Shedd says

---

30  W. Graham Scroggie, *Paul's Prison Prayers* (1921, rprt.; Grand Rapids: Kregel Publications, 1981).

31  Donald Crogin, *The Prayers of the New Testament* (New York: Harper and Row, Publishers, 1967).

32  Herbert Lockyer, *All the Prayers of the Bible* (Grand Rapids: Zondervan Publishing House, 1959). Thankfully while books treating public prayers have neglected the use of Scripture-language, the books on private prayer have not. Pratt's is especially good in this respect.

33  Willimon, *Preaching and Leading Worship*, 44; see also Johnson, *Leading in Worship*, 41.

34  Fairburn, *Pastoral Theology*, 318; Murphy, *Pastoral Theology*, 207.

the minister "ought to study *method* in prayer, and observe it. A prayer should have a plan as much as a sermon."[35]

Likewise, R.L. Dabney urges, "I deem that the minister is as much bound to prepare himself for praying in public as for preaching. The negligence with which many preachers leave their prayers to accident, while they lay out all their strength on their sermons, is most painfully suggestive of unbelief toward God and indifference to the edification of their brethren." He labels the idea that one should trust in the leading of the Holy Spirit in prayer rather than prepare ahead of time "a remnant of fanatical enthusiasm." "To speak for God to men is a sacred and responsible task. To speak for men to God is not less responsible, and is more solemn… The young minister should no more venture into the pulpit with an *impromptu* prayer, than with an *impromptu* sermon."[36] Both Dabney and Miller (like Murphy) encourage the discipline of what they call "devotional composition," meaning "not so much to recite these written prayers in the pulpit," explains Dabney, "as to train his own taste, and to gather a store of devotional language."[37] Among modern writers, Robert Rayburn agrees: "If a minister wishes to be effective in leading the prayers of his congregation he must prepare for his public prayers."[38]

## Brief

Third, public prayers should be brief. Do not try the patience of God's people by rambling on and on. Even the nineteenth-century writers recommend brevity. Murphy recommends that the main prayer should be five minutes, or no more than eight. Samuel Miller complains of the "excessive length" of some

---

35 Shedd, *Homiletics*, 271.

36 Dabney, *Sacred Rhetoric*, 346-7, 360.

37 Ibid., 360; see also Miller, *Public Prayer*, 288ff.

38 Rayburn, *O Come Let Us Worship*, 199.

prayers.[39] Planning helps to ensure brevity. Careful preparation will help avoid the "verbiage and repetition" about which Shedd complains.[40] It will also guard against the frequent and mechanical repetition of favorite phrases, titles of God, and any other formula of words, of which Dabney complains.[41] He writes, "This mechanical phrase is obnoxious to every charge of formalism, monotony and lack of appropriate variety, which we lodge against an unchangeable liturgy, while it has none of its literary merit and dignified and tender associations."[42] Wandering prayers, meandering at length here, there, and everywhere, will also be corrected by preparation.

## Undiluted

Fourth, maintain the integrity of public prayer as prayer. Don't use the occasions of prayer as opportunities to do other things. To that end, pray, don't preach. Dabney warns of the "painful absurdity in our going about formally to instruct God of his doctrinal truth," or our seeming "to preach to God instead of praying to him."[43] Shedd warns of "didactically discoursing in prayer."[44] Murphy calls it "a great abuse of public prayer to use it for preaching to the audience or for rebuking them, or even, as is often done, for giving information to the Lord."[45] *Pray, don't announce.* Many of us will have heard ministers pray, "Lord, we thank you for the prayer meeting which is held in the chapel on Wednesday evening at seven o'clock, just after the fellowship supper and just before choir rehearsal. And we know that you want all your people to come unless providentially hindered.

---

39 Miller, *Public Prayer*, 187.

40 Shedd, *Homiletics*, 272-3.

41 Dabney, *Sacred Rhetoric*, 347-8.

42 Ibid., 348.

43 Ibid., 355.

44 Shedd, *Homiletics*, 273.

45 Murphy, *Pastoral Theology*, 211-212.

Help us to make it a priority." This is "a great abuse of public prayer" (not to mention silly), and must be avoided.

## Appropriate

Fifth, use appropriate terminology. Choose suitable language in addressing the Almighty. The old authors denounce, with surprising vehemence, the use of over-familiar language in prayer. "Familiarity is the worst of faults in prayer," says Shedd.[46] Dabney heaps scorn on "Half-educated or spiritually proud men" who "frequently indulge in an indecent familiarity with the Most High, under the pretense of filial nearness and importunity."[47] Spurgeon counsels that one avoid "an unhallowed and sickening superabundance of endearing words." He says, "When 'Dear Lord,' and 'Blessed Lord,' and 'Sweet Lord,' come over and over again as vain repetitions, they are among the worst of blots." He wishes that "in some way or other," those who indulge such "fond and familiar expressions" could come "to a better understanding of the true relation existing between man and God."[48] He counsels that one be "scrupulously reverent" in one's language.[49]

## Full diet

Sixth, pray a "full-diet" (Hughes Old terminology) of biblical prayer.[50] The Reformation was not only a revolution in preaching, a revolution in church song, and an eucharistic revolution, it was also a revolution in prayer. On the basis of the study of Scripture and the church fathers, the Reformers identified six basic prayer

---

46  Shedd, *Homiletics*, 273.

47  Dabney, *Sacred Rhetoric*, 349.

48  Spurgeon, *Lectures*, 57.

49  Ibid., 58.

50  See Hughes O. Old, *Worship that is Reformed According to Scripture* (1984; 2nd ed., Louisville: Westminster/John Knox Press, 2004), 173.

genres, all of which became a part of their regular orders of worship.[51] These were:

| | |
|---|---|
| Praise | Intercession |
| Confession of Sin | Illumination |
| Thanksgiving | Benediction |

In addition, they identified (especially from 1 Tim. 2:1-3) a "five-fold" focus of the church's intercessions likewise featured in their orders of service:

Sanctification of the saints
Church and its ministry
Sick and destitute
Civil authorities and the nation
Christian mission around the world

This reform represents a substantial commitment to public prayer, vastly increasing what was typical of the medieval liturgies or became normative in the Tridentine Mass.[52] A church that believes in *sola fide* will fill its public services with Scripture and a church that believes in *sola gratia* will fill its services with prayer. "If we are to have souls saved," C. H. Spurgeon insists, "we must pray: we must pray: we must pray."[53]

**Clear headings**
Fifth, maintain clear categories and clear transitions in prayer. This is particularly important if one's service includes a "pastoral" or "great prayer" that incorporates confession of sin and the five-

---

51  Eg. Strasburg (Bucer), Geneva (Calvin), Edinburgh (Knox), etc.; and later, the *Westminster Directory*. See Johnson, *Worshipping with Calvin*, 39-43, 111-122.

52  Roman Catholic services prior to Vatican II featured only the prayer of confession of sin and eucharistic prayers as part of the ordinary liturgy. The other genres were missing.

53  Cited in Iain H. Murray, *Heroes* (Edinburgh: The Banner of Truth Trust, 2009), 289; from his *Speeches at Home and Abroad* (1878).

fold intercessions. Too often, public prayer sounds as though it is nothing more than a random collection of unconnected devotional thoughts. Recognize that stream-of-consciousness praying is likely to be no more effective than stream-of-consciousness preaching. If there is no order in prayer, the congregation will struggle to pray along with the one praying. They wonder (as congregations often ask of disordered preaching) "where is he going" or worse, they will check out altogether. Clear transitions are essential. "We confess our sins… we pray for our sanctification… we pray for the church and its ministry… we pray for the sick… we pray for the nation…. We pray for Christian mission… and we pray as we open your Word for the illumination of the Holy Spirit." Maintain clear, pronounced categories and transitions.

## EXAMPLE

It remains for us now to illustrate the way in which such prayers are actually prayed, and apply the above principles to the five major prayers of the worship service. As the minister *invokes* the presence of God, he should fill his praise with the language of Scripture. The congregation needs to hear him humbly exalting the greatness and majesty of God. Remember that they are likely to learn how to pray in large part from listening to their minister. Study the great prayers of praise and glean from the Psalms their rich devotional expressions. Week by week provide for them a vision of the power and glory and goodness of the God whom they worship, a God for whom nothing is impossible, a God who can do all things, and God to whom homage and adoration is due.

As the minister moves on to the *prayer of confession*, he should use the deep, prolonged, detailed language of Scripture. The people of God come to church each week bruised and battered by sin. They come burdened with guilt, knowing something of what they ought to be and their failure. Let them hear their minister humbly grieving for sin on their behalf as you confess idolatry, greed, covetousness, pride, lust, selfishness, jealousy, envy and gossip. Let him confess that God has not been loved with all our heart, mind, soul and strength and we've not loved our neighbor as ourselves. Use, for example, the language of David and confess,

> I know my transgressions, and my sin is ever before me. Against you, you only, have I sinned, and done what is evil in your sight. I was brought forth in iniquity, and in sin my mother conceived me.

And then begin to plead with David,

> Be gracious to us, O God, according to your lovingkindness; according to the greatness of your compassion blot out our transgressions. Wash us thoroughly from our iniquity, and cleanse us from our sin. Purify us with hyssop, and we shall be clean; wash us and we shall be whiter than snow. Hide your face from our sins, and blot out all our iniquities. Deliver us from blood guiltiness, O God, the God of our salvation. Create in us clean hearts, O God, and renew a steadfast spirit within us. Restore to us the joy of your salvation, and sustain us with a willing spirit. O Lord, open our lips, that our mouth may declare your praise (Ps. 51).

The people of God are struggling to believe the gospel and struggling to experience forgiveness. They may have confessed their sin privately, and yet they have not found relief. Often, the problem is that they have not gone deeply enough. Their brokenness has been healed superficially with flippant promises that "'all is well, all is well;' but there is no peace" (Jer. 8:11). They need to hear their minister earnestly acknowledging and grieving sin and claiming the promises of God on their behalf. I mentioned hating the Prayer Book my first six months in Britain. Eventually

I learned to love it and even looked forward to going to chapel each day, in no small part so that I could pray Cranmer's beautiful general confession. I found it "therapeutic," though I hesitate to use the word, to deal with God with my sins in congregational worship each day. This is what people need to experience in our worship. They need to deal with God. Their minister needs to lead them there with praise and then confession. Let them hear him conclude his confession with a rehearsal of the promises of God. Give thanks for the promise of 1 John 1:9, that if we confess our sins, God is faithful and just to forgive us our sins and to cleanse us from all unrighteousness. Give thanks that Jesus "bore our sins in His body on the cross" (1 Pet. 2:24 NASB); that "He gave His life a ransom for many" (Matt. 20:28 NASB); that though He knew no sin He became sin "that we might become the righteousness of God in Him" (2 Cor. 5:21). Give thanks that we now have "no condemnation" and "peace with God" in Christ (Rom. 8:1; 5:1). Even pray for them the extended promises of Psalm 103:8, 10-12.

As the service moves into a time of intercessions, plead for the sanctification of the people; let them hear compassion and urgency in their minister as he prays that the ideals of the Christian life might be realized in their lives. They need to hear him praying week after week that they might be holy even as God is holy (1 Pet. 1:15-16), that they might be imitators of God as beloved children, and walk in love (Eph 5:1ff), and conformed to the image of Christ, bearing the fruit of the Spirit (Gal. 5:22-23). Let them hear him pleading that they'll not love the world nor the things of the world, and that they'll not be seduced by the lust of the eyes, the lust of the flesh, and the boastful pride of life (1 John 2:15-16).

Move on then into four other areas of intercession (mentioned above) found in Scripture, used by the early church, and revived by the Reformers. Pray, one, for the the church's ministry (Matt. 9:36-38; 1 Tim. 2:1-2); two, for the afflicted (2 Cor. 1:3-4, 11; James 5:13-18); three, for the civil authorities and the nation; and four, for the Christian mission around the world – "all man" (1 Tim. 2:1, 3-4).[54] They need to hear the breadth of their minister's prayers. They need to hear his prayers circle the globe as he prays for the progress of Christian missions, for ministers and missionaries, for the nation, and for the needy.

What about the prayer of illumination? Doesn't the congregation need to be reminded that "the natural person does not accept the things of the Spirit of God" (1 Cor. 2:14)? Won't the people of God benefit from a weekly reminder that they are dependent upon the Holy Spirit if they are ever to understand the Word of God? Pray for illumination before reading Scripture and/or before preaching. Pray that eyes will be opened, (Ps. 119:18) that ears will be unstopped, that stony hearts will be replaced with hearts of flesh, that stiff-necks will be loosened. Pray that the eyes of the heart might be enlightened (Eph. 3:18), that the Lord might teach us His truth (Ps. 86:11-12), and give us understanding (Ps. 119:33).

Finally, they need to hear their minister pray the blessing of God upon them. Bless them with the Apostolic benediction (2 Cor. 13:14) or the Aaronic (Num. 6:24-26) or some other (e.g. Heb. 13:20-21). Let them leave with one of these scriptural blessings ringing in their ears. Will that not encourage them as they leave? Does this not conclude the service on the gospel's optimistic note?

Is it now clear why we have said that the minister needs to lead in prayer? Who in the congregation is trained to pray in this manner? Who is most aware of the pastoral needs of the congregation? Who has been set apart for three years of biblical and theological education? Who spends extended time each day in the study of Scripture? Who labors daily on his knees in private prayer for the souls of the saints? Who consequently is capable of praying in the rich devotional language of Scripture as well

---

54 Johnson, *Leading in Worship*, 10n15; 34n4; 52-54.

as in a manner that is theologically sound? Public prayer is not merely a matter of the minister or anyone else standing up and praying off the top of their heads. The first thing into most of our minds, as Spurgeon once said, is "mere froth." Even as it makes sense to have the minister preach and administer the sacraments, it makes sense to have him pray. The prayers that we envision are those offered by a man called by God, who saturates his mind with the Word of God, and spends hours each week on his knees before God. Even as the church has deemed it wise to apply the New Testament admonitions to "guard the gospel" by entrusting its proclamation through Word and Sacrament only to those ordained to do so, so also it is both pastorally and theologically wise to leave leadership in prayer in the hands of the minister.

Has public prayer been given the attention it deserves? Do we now understand how public prayer is a means of grace that builds the church? Begin now to practice "studied prayer," as the Puritans called it, or to employ Watts' term, "conceived prayer." Plan the church's public prayers, fill them with scriptural language and allusions, and watch the sanctifying impact that they make upon the congregation multiply to the glory of God.

# 4

# Leading in Preaching

There are a number of superb books available on preaching, none of which we pretend to improve upon. My favorites are those by William Still, Spurgeon, and Lloyd-Jones.[1] We cannot commend them too highly. Among the most fruitful studies that one can undertake to shape a preaching ministry is to read and reread those works. What we rather hope to do is just offer a few suggestions based on over thirty-five years of ordained ministry. My suggestions also reflect our work with pastoral interns over as many years and our concern for what we perceive to be weaknesses in their seminary training.

## LECTIO CONTINUA

First, preach the *lectio continua*. That is, *preach expositorily and sequentially*. Always preach a text of Scripture. Beyond that, commit to preaching verse-by-verse through whole books of the Bible. The Reformation can be said to have started for the Reformed churches when, in January 1519, Zwingli removed

---

1 William Still, *The Work of the Pastor* (1965; Fearn, Ross-shire: Christian Focus Publications, 2010), C. H. Spurgeon, *Lectures to My Students* (1881; Edinburgh: Banner of Truth Trust, 2008); D. Martyn Lloyd-Jones, *Preaching and Preachers* (Grand Rapids, MI: Zondervan, 1971).

his clerical garb, abandoned the lectionary, and began to preach through the book of Matthew. In doing this, he was merely following the pattern that he saw in the greatest of the church fathers, including Origen, Gregory of Nazianzus, Gregory the Great, and, for immediate inspiration, Augustine's sermons on John and Chrysostom's on Matthew. The abandonment of the *lectio selecta* in favor of the *lectio continua* was an early mark of the Reformed churches and according to Hughes Old, "unquestionably one of the most clear restorations of the form of worship of the early Church."[2] Not only Zwingli, but Luther, Bucer, Oecolampadius, Calvin, the Scottish Reformers, and the English Puritans all were committed to expository, sequential preaching, though in the latter case the pace often slowed to that of the proverbial snail. We can say as well that it has been the commitment of the church in virtually every era of health and vitality throughout its long history.

We are sorry to report that there seems to be a waning commitment to expository preaching among Reformed ministers, and particularly among recent seminary graduates. Years ago, one of the fathers of the Presbyterian Church of America (PCA), Dr. James Baird (1928–2020), himself a practitioner of expository preaching, explained that few men were doing so any more. I was surprised when he said it and wasn't sure that he had it quite right. Now, I am certain that he did. Why is this happening? One of my interns told me that he was afraid he would not find anything interesting in "the next text," and might be thought boring by the people. A healthy fear of boring the people is not necessarily a bad thing to carry with one throughout one's ministry. It may help keep one sharp. However, what was he saying about God's self-revelation in Scripture? Boring? I'm sure that he really didn't mean to be saying that, yet I am also sure

---

2 Old, *Patristic Roots*, 195.

that he was merely expressing what many others fear deep down inside: the Bible alone is dull.

I responded by insisting he begin preaching through the book of Philippians. Halfway through his preparation for the first sermon, he came to me full of anxiety that he would have nothing to say about the first four verses. I smiled and urged him to press on. On the day of the sermon, he came back to me brimming with enthusiasm, saying that he had twice as much to say as he could in the allotted time and would only make it to the second verse. This experience repeated itself several times, and on each occasion, he emerged more enthusiastic than the previous. Today, he is a zealous and capable expository preacher, pastoring one of the premier churches of the PCA.

The basic conviction that is lacking and which I commend to you is that Christ is found in "all the Scriptures" (Luke 24:27). The whole Christ is found in the whole Bible, as William Still would say, and we only become whole people when we feed on the whole Christ. Our responsibility is to preach "all Scripture," since "all Scripture" is "inspired by God," and consequently is "profitable for teaching, for reproof, for correction, for training in righteousness, that the man of God may be adequate, equipped for every good work" (2 Tim. 3:16-17 NASB). I take the word "all" to mean that there are no exceptions. It is all profitable, even if it is not all equally accessible. We may not deprive our congregations of any of it. The "whole counsel of God" is to be proclaimed, even as the Apostle Paul did at Ephesus (Acts 20:27).

Commitment to *lectio continua* preaching raises the question of one's *real* doctrine of inspiration, whatever might be *claimed*. Did God give to us "all the Scriptures?" Are they all "profitable?" Are they able to give us "the wisdom that leads to salvation through faith which is in Christ Jesus" (2 Tim. 3:15 NASB)? Then it is the minister's job to preach all of it, on each occasion discerning why God included those verses in the canon and the profit He wishes His people to derive from them. A sermon, as Old concludes from Nehemiah 8:8, "is not just a lecture on some religious subject, it is rather an explanation of a passage of Scripture."[3] The media has had a negative impact in this respect. It is not the pastor's job to be "exciting" or "entertaining." As we have mentioned, too much preaching has come to resemble the sound bites, or, more accurately, the rapidly moving images of video screens. Story follows illustration follows anecdote follows joke follows story follows illustration, etc. Scripture takes a back seat to "relevance" and the preacher's ego. The Apostle Paul repudiates this kind of spruced-up proclamation, preferring "the foolishness of preaching," even if such were despised by rhetorical form-conscious Greek orators (1 Cor. 1:21). Listen to his language and evaluate the contemporary stress on style in the light of it.

> And I, when I came to you, brothers, did not come proclaiming to you the testimony of God with lofty speech or wisdom. For I decided to know nothing among you except Jesus Christ and him crucified. And I was with you in weakness and in fear and much trembling, and my speech and my message were not in plausible words of wisdom, but in demonstration of the Spirit and of power, so that your faith might not rest in the wisdom of men but in the power of God (1 Cor. 2:1-5).

The Apostle's conviction is that the gospel, or "the word of the cross" is the power of God (Rom. 1:16; 1 Cor. 1:18). He is not concerned to clothe his message with "plausible words of wisdom." He doesn't mind preaching "in weakness and in fear and in much trembling." Indeed, he is convinced that this is the way that he must preach. If he were to dress up either his "message" (content) or "preaching" (form) in "plausibly words of

---

3 Old, *Worship*, 60.

wisdom" then his hearers might place their faith in him, in "the wisdom of men" rather than on "the power of God."

Insofar as there is a crisis in preaching, it is a crisis of confidence in the converting and sanctifying power of the Word of God. Do we believe that God saves sinners through His Word? Do we believe that the gospel is "the power of God for salvation" (Rom. 1:16)? Do we believe that God is "well-pleased ... to save those who believe" through "the foolishness of preaching" (1 Cor. 1:21 NASB)? Do we believe that "the Spirit of God maketh the reading, but especially the preaching, of the Word, an effectual means of convincing and converting sinners, and of building them up in holiness and comfort, through faith, unto salvation" (*Shorter Catechism* 89)? Then preach it … all of it.

## TEXTUAL

Second, *preach the text*. We make a subtle but important point. Preach the text, not a topic from the text. It is not enough to find a doctrine in the text and preach that doctrine, even if it is preached with great competence. The minister must first show his listeners, more than that, convince them that *his* text teaches *that* doctrine. Prove it to them. They are not interested in his opinions and theories. There is no spiritual power in his stories and illustrations. Show them that the text teaches that doctrine and so they must believe it and do what it says.

Again, my interns have helped me to see this problem. They would read their text, announce what it means, and then spend the next twenty-nine minutes talking about their subject without again referring to the text. This way of preaching is not nearly so effective as demonstrating clearly that the subject at hand is actually there in the passage before them. John MacArthur is something of a genius at doing this. He is constantly forcing his listeners to look at the text and deal with what it says. He reads it and comments. He reads it again with more emphasis.

He tells you what it says. Then he tells you what it doesn't say. He asks you questions about what it says. "God so loved the world that He *what*?" he asks. "Who will not perish? 'Whosoever believeth.' Who does *that* include? Does that include me? Yes. You? Yes. That rich man? That poor man? That white man? That black man? Yes. '*Whosoever believeth*,' it says. Even a thief? Yes. A murderer? A philanderer? A pimp? '*Whosoever!*'" Explain, emphasize, elaborate upon, illustrate your text! Don't wander off and tell us everything you know about the subject, and every story you know remotely related to the subject. Teach us the text. Keep leading us back to the text. The preacher must show that the truth he preaches is "a truth contained in or grounded on that text," says the Westminster *Directory for the Publick Worship of God* (1645), "that the hearers may discern how God teacheth it *from thence*" (my emphasis).

## WITHOUT FORMULAS

Third, *avoid formulas.* History has its schools of preaching. There are a number of advocates of one or another method today. A sermon always begins like this, they say, then it does this, and finally it ends like this. Some will assume that one must always begin with an attention-grabbing opening statement, develop the body of the sermon, and then always, always, always end on a positive note, with what we might call the Reformed altar call, consisting of a heavy dose of grace and forgiveness and hope. We have one question for this kind of thinking: where do we find this in the Bible? The Bible itself presents its contents with grand variety. There is no cookie cutter. There is no formula. Sometimes it crushes us. Sometimes it comforts us. The minister's job is to preach his text. The text determines both the form and content of your message. This means that no single sermonic method will work. The preacher must let his text speak for itself, with its emphasis being its own. Certainly, we always preach in the context of the whole

Bible and gospel message. The threat of judgment is proclaimed in light of the gospel call to repentance and promise of salvation. Yet the preacher should take care not to blunt the edge of his text. The message of the verses being preached should not die the death of a thousand qualifications. The people need to hear the warnings of the New Testament unfiltered. The threats, "Whatsoever a man soweth that shall he also reap," "Those who practice such things shall not enter the kingdom of God," "Depart from Me I never knew you," need to fall on the ears of God's people without them being explained away in the name of grace (Gal. 6:7, 5:21; Matt. 7:21ff). The Apostles did not hesitate to address such threats to the people of God and neither should we. They did not hesitate to connect God's blessings to the conditions of faithfulness and obedience, and neither should we (e.g. Matt. 7:7-8; 1 John 1:6-10; James 4:1-3, 7-10; Eph. 6:1-3, etc.). Likewise, every gracious promise need not be "balanced" by a reminder of the need of faithfulness and obedience. A preacher should not feel obligated to drag in James 2 every time he preaches on John 3:16 or Ephesians 2:8-9. Let the text speak!

## ASSUME IGNORANCE

Fourth, *assume that no one knows anything*. I find that young preachers tend to preach as though their audience were bringing to the table far more knowledge than is typically the case. Seminarians and recent graduates are pumped full of knowledge and seem to forget that relatively few know what they now know. This is especially true of those who are more theologically or philosophically oriented. I have heard discussions of "worldview" that have been aimed way over the heads of most in the congregation. The young preacher was excited about what he knew, yet no one else knew what he was talking about. Several times I have heard my interns launch into a critique of contemporary evangelicalism among people who know nothing of the personalities and issues involved. Lacking that context, their criticisms were irrelevant, if not incomprehensible. Others will speak of Paul and the Judaizers, Jesus and the Pharisees, Philippi, the temple, and so on, and assume everyone knows what they are referring to. A few years back, I preached through Galatians. At one point I had been talking about Judaizers for weeks and was ready to launch into my sermon about the Judaizers this and Judaizers that when I saw a couple in the front row whom I knew to be unbelievers. On the spot, I decided to talk for half a minute or so about salvation by faith in Christ apart from works. I then described who the various parties involved were before finally jumping into the middle of Paul's argument in Galatians 3. It didn't take long. Yet I had to set the stage or else I'd lose our visitors right off the bat.

## EXPLAIN CONTEXT

Fifth, *explain the context but don't dwell on it.* I respect the strengths of the redemptive-historical approach to preaching. I think that one should provide historical-biblical-theological context in one's message. Yet I don't think that there is much value in dwelling on it. By "dwelling on it," I mean talking for fifteen minutes or more in a thirty-minute sermon about what was "long ago and far away," as Jay Adams would put it. After all, the point of understanding what God did for *them* back then is so that we can understand what He is doing today *for us*. Tell me what the text means for me today. Spurgeon talks about making a beeline for the cross from whatever text he preaches. That is exactly what we mean. Bring the passage to bear upon the present in a hurry. To that end, we recommend that preachers not wait for the end of the sermon to make application. Draw points of application out of each sub-point of the sermon, the way that Matthew Henry does in his commentary on the whole Bible. Apply as you go along. More about this in a moment.

## REVIEW AND REPEAT

Sixth, *review and repeat constantly*. Learn to say the same thing five different ways like the Apostle Paul does in Galatians 2:16 (NASB):

> Nevertheless knowing that a man is not justified by the works of the Law but through faith in Christ Jesus, even we have believed in Christ Jesus, that we may be justified by faith in Christ, and not by the works of the Law; since by the works of the Law shall no flesh be justified.

He says that we are justified by faith not five but six times in one verse! He says it negatively, positively, and every which way. Scripture constantly does this. It can talk about the circumcised heart, about regeneration, about being born again, about being baptized by the Spirit, about being a new creation. The Bible says the same things over and over again, but does so in a dozen different ways. Again, John MacArthur is a genius at this. He'll say, "You must *repent*. You must *turn* from your sins. You must tell God that you *are sorry*. You must *give up* the old ways." We mustn't say the same things the same ways. Then people will lose interest. Rather, say the same thing with variety, using both simple and sophisticated vocabulary so as to appeal to all. "What does the Bible say about *eschatology*? What does it say about the *end times*? Can we know what will happen at the *end of the world*? What does it teach us about the *last days*?"

Not only should we use repetition, but also review constantly. Review the main headings periodically. Tell the congregation what has been said so it can better understand where the sermon is going. Even the best listeners can miss major points and lose touch with the direction of the sermon. It helps if the preacher says periodically, "Here is what we have seen so far. First … Second… Third… Now, fourth we see that he says …" This allows everyone to catch up, to see again how the whole sermon hangs together, and may even help the minister to realize where he is going! More than once, I have finally realized my main point in the process of such a review. A quick review helps everyone.

## APPLICATION

Seventh, *apply the text.* This brings us back to something that we said earlier. The application is in the text! There is a reason why each passage of Scripture is in the canon. John said that the whole world couldn't contain all that might have been written about Jesus (John 21:25). Consequently, a purposeful editorial hand was at work including and excluding according to God's purposes for the church. Answer the question as to why a text is there, and we have the application. "This passage is here so that we might believe or do what?" Constantly ask and answer that question. Dr. Baird used to tell me to answer the question, "So what?" every five minutes. Think of that businessman out there who is tempted to check his phone for news or messages. Keep his attention. Show him the relevance of your text. The relevance is there. Tell him what it is frequently. I recall as a seminary student preparing to preach and struggling to make applications. My problem was that I was trying to manufacture them out of thin air. Application is not difficult. It is always there in the text, sometimes explicitly, as in the epistles, and sometimes implicitly, as in historical narrative, but it is always there. For example, how does one apply Philippians 4:6-7 (NASB)?

> Be anxious for nothing, but in everything by prayer and supplication with thanksgiving let your requests be made known to God. And the peace of God, which surpasses all comprehension, shall guard your hearts and your minds in Christ Jesus.

Assuming that one has already provided the background and meaning of the text, one helps the congregation to understand why they worry. Help them to identify anxiety and its sources. Then direct them to prayer as the solution, explaining how the various elements of prayer address the problem of anxiety. Isn't that the Apostle Paul's point? Isn't he telling them not to be anxious but instead to pray, and that the result will be peace? Since it is his point, shouldn't it be yours? Sinclair Ferguson says, "We shortchange our hearers by failing to show how the application of Scripture arises from and is usually given with the very passage we are expounding."[4]

## BREVITY

Eighth, *preach short sermons*. Some concessions must be made to our pictographic culture if our people are to thrive under expository preaching week after week. Even a weak preacher can be effective if he restricts himself to half an hour. Less than thirty minutes is too much like a "sermonette," which, as John Stott says, breeds "Christianettes." However, if a preacher is going to preach more than thirty minutes, he had better be good – real good. Luis Palau could preach for an hour. John MacArthur can preach for forty-five minutes. If after two or three years of regular preaching the people are crying out for longer sermons, go ahead and extend the time. Lacking that, it is best that we keep it short.

## URGENCY

Ninth, *preach with urgency*. We've mentioned leading worship services with a sense of urgency. Preach in the same way. Study the text so as to become convinced of the message that God has for His people in that passage. Once we know what God is saying, there ought to be a great urgency about communicating

---

4  Sinclair Ferguson, "Evangelical Exemplar," *Tabletalk*, Feb. 1999.

His message. After all, God is speaking. Eternity is at stake. We can't drone on as though we were lecturing a captive audience. A sense of urgency ought to animate all that we say. Reformed Baptist minister, Al Martin, once remarked, "A man who yells 'fire' from a burning building has a natural eloquence." Do we believe that there is a fire? Do we believe that souls are in danger? Then our voice and manner will take on a natural eloquence. True eloquence cannot be contrived. It cannot be manufactured through a classroom course on elocution. Rather, it is the result of the passion that is born of conviction regarding the great themes of time and eternity. Because the truths of the Reformed faith (really, of the Christian faith) are interrelated and interdependent, it is possible to be convinced every time that we go into the pulpit that we are preaching the most important of messages. How many times did Martin Lloyd-Jones begin a sermon saying, "I am going to speak to you tonight about the most important subject in all the world." He believed he was, because he saw at a glance the interrelatedness of all of truth. The preacher should not enter the pulpit until he is convinced that he has a message from God that is vital for the people of God. Every time he preaches, he should carry with him the burden of knowing that the people of God must know what his text teaches and understand its implications. Listen to Richard Baxter as he urges "close and lively application" of the Word of God in preaching.

> O sirs, how plainly, how closely, how earnestly, should we deliver a message of such moment as ours, when the everlasting life or everlasting death of our fellow-men is involved in it!... Remember they must be awakened or damned, and that a sleepy preacher will hardly awaken drowsy sinners. Though you give the holy things of God the highest praises in words, yet, if you do it coldly, you will seem by your manner to unsay what you said in the matter. It is a kind of contempt of great things,

especially of so great things, to speak of them without much affection and fervency.[5]

## AUTHENTIC

Tenth, *be yourself*. Phillips Brooks defined preaching as "truth through personality."[6] We have noticed amongst some of our colleagues in the ministry a regrettable transformation as they make the transition from small group study to the pulpit. In the small group they are animated, interesting, engaging, in a word, they are themselves. Their personalities shine in that setting, enhancing and enlivening their teaching. Yet when they walk into the pulpit, they change. Their personality disappears. They seem bound-up, unnatural, stiff. They are not themselves, and as a result, they are not nearly as effective as they could be. Some younger men make the mistake of trying to be Rev. So and So, Junior. They mimic their hero's style, his phrases, his manner, his illustrations, and so on. Rarely will this work. He is not that person. He cannot preach just like the Rev. Sr. does. Young preachers can learn from other preachers. Indeed, good preaching is as much caught as taught. Yet he mustn't try to be the other man. He can't be. He can be himself on fire, but not someone else. His aim must be to so immerse himself in his text that he is moved to become an enlivened, animated, eloquent version of himself. Let the text preach to the preacher first. As it does, it will inspire thoughts and phrases that are natural. It will inspire illustrations that arise organically from his own experience. This is why illustrations from books of illustrations rarely work well. They are not personal. We cannot preach someone else's experience. A preacher can only preach effectively

---

5  Richard Baxter, *The Reformed Pastor* (1656, rprt; Edinburgh: The Banner of Truth Trust, 1974), 147-48.

6  Phillips Brooks, *Lectures on Preaching Delivered before the Divinity School of Yale College In January and February, 1887* (New York: E.P. Dutton and Company, 1907), 5.

his own experience. Let the truth fire the heart and language and illustrations will come. Then, because the content has come naturally, it will be easier to deliver the sermon naturally. Don't try to be someone else. A preacher must use the gifts that God has given him, and be himself.

## EXHORTATION

Eleventh, *don't forget exhortation*. By this, I mean more than application. Those who have heard the meaning of the text explained, and have heard of its application for today, must be exhorted to believe and implement all that the text requires of them.

Richard Baxter and Jonathan Edwards from long ago – and Martin Lloyd-Jones of recent memory – were particularly effective at this. Baxter preached with what Packer called "hands and feet," walking and clawing all over his hearers, urging, pleading, exhorting. His "Treatise on Conversion" is extraordinary in this respect. For sustained, passionate pleading and persuading it is nearly beyond belief. Both Edwards and Lloyd-Jones had a way of getting inside one's head, anticipating one's questions and objections, stating them better than one could oneself, and then demolishing them. Read Edwards' "Men Are Naturally God's Enemies." Every possible objection to the thesis of his title is answered as he pleads for all to come to Christ. Read any of Lloyd-Jones' sermons. In his sermon mentioned previously, in which he attacked the Calvinistic preachers, he said things like this:

> You've become timid about the free offer of the gospel. You are afraid of sounding like an Arminian and that is a thing abhorrent to you. But listen to the Apostle Paul – 'save yourselves from this wicked generation,' he says. 'Save yourselves!' But you've become learned. You've become a theologian. You read books. You've read the Puritans, and are now an intellectual. But where

is your fire? 'Your Calvinistic preachers are boring,' a lady told me with regret. I had to admit that she was right. We're quoting the Reformers. We're quoting the Puritans. We're quoting the Princeton theologians and our people don't know what we're talking about. Lord have mercy upon us!

Lloyd-Jones is all over us. He is pleading. He is exhorting. He is urging. This is what we must be doing.

> Why won't you believe? Because the gospel lacks evidence? Go on now. It is not an intellectual problem, now is it? The problem is moral, not intellectual. You don't want to believe. You don't want to give up your lifestyle. You don't want God telling you what to do. You want to be your own man, the captain of your own ship. But where has that gotten you? Your life is a mess, isn't it? You're empty.

Go after them. Make generous use of the second person, as Peter does in Acts 2: "Jesus Christ whom *you* crucified." Plead, urge, exhort. Work on the congregation from every angle, repeating your text, urging their compliance, answering their objections. Don't let anyone escape.

\*\*\*

This then is how we think the public ministry ought to be conducted. Each service must be carefully planned. Know why we are doing what we are doing, and how transitions are going to be made. Strive to create a mood of "reverence and awe," approaching each succeeding element of worship with sobriety and urgency. Bathe the service with Scripture. Pray, read, sing, and preach the language of the Bible. Public worship will make or break a minister's ministry. In the church's public services, the preacher has before him his primary spiritual responsibility. In these services, he has the means of grace. Diligently use those means and prove to be a workman who need not be ashamed.

# Suggested Reading

## WORSHIP

Cruse, Jonathan Landry. *What Happens When We Worship.* Grand Rapids: Reformation Heritage Books, 2020.

Hageman, H. G. *Pulpit & Table: Some Chapters in the History of Worship in the Reformed Churches.* Richmond, Virginia: John Knox Press, 1962.

Hart, D.G. *Recovering Mother Kirk: The Case for Liturgy in the Reformed Tradition.* Grand Rapids, Michigan: Baker Book House, 2003.

Hart, D. G. and John R. Muether. *With Reverence and Awe: Returning to the Basics of Reformed Worship.* Phillipsburg, NJ: P&R Publishing, 2002.

Horton, Michael. *A Better Way: Rediscovering the Drama of God-Centered Worship.* Grand Rapids, Michigan: Baker Books, 2002.

Johnson, Terry L. *Contemporary Worship.* Edinburgh, Scotland: The Banner of Truth Trust, 2014.

_____. *Leading in Worship.* 1996; Durham, UK: EP Books, 2019.

_____. *Reformed Worship: Worship that Is According to Scripture.* Welwyn Garden City, UK: EP Books, 2015.

_____. *Serving with Calvin.* Welwyn Garden City, UK: EP Books, 2015.

_____. *Worshipping with Calvin.* Darlington, England: EP Books, 2014.

Macleod, Donald. *Presbyterian Worship: Its Developments and Forms.* Richmond: John Knox Press, 1965.

Maxwell, William D. *An Outline of Christian Worship: Its Developments and Forms.* 1936; London: Oxford University Press, 1952.

Merton, Julius. *Presbyterian Worship in America.* Richmond: John Knox Press, 1967.

Mueller, Richard A. and Rowland S. Ward. *Scripture and Worship: Biblical Interpretation and the Directory for Public Worship.* Phillipsburg, NJ: P&R Publishing, 2007.

Nicols, James Hastings. *Corporate Worship in the Reformed Tradition.* Philadelphia, Pennsylvania: The Westminster Press, 1968.

Old, Hughes Oliphant. *Themes and Variations for a Christian Doxology.* Grand Rapids: Eerdmans, 1992.

Old, Hughes Oliphant. *The Patristic Roots of Reformed Worship.* Zurich: Theologischer Verlag, 1970.

Old, Hughes Oliphant. *Worship That Is Reformed According to Scriptures (Guides to the Reformed Tradition).* Atlanta: John Knox Press, 1984.

Payne, Jon D. *In the Splendor of Holiness.* White Hall, WV: Tolle Lege Press, 2008.

Rayburn, Robert. *O' Come Let Us Worship.* Grand Rapids: Baker Book House, 1980.

Ryken, Philip G., Derek W. H. Thomas, and J. Ligon Duncan, III (eds.). *Give Praise to God: A Vision for Reforming Worship.* Phillipsburg, New Jersey: P&R Publishing, 2003.

Ryle, J.C. *Worship: Its Priority, Principles, & Practice.* Edinburgh: The Banner of Truth Trust, 2005.

Von Allmen, J.-J. *Worship: Its Theology and Practice.* London: Lutterworth Press, 1965.

## PASTORAL PRACTICE

Baxter, Richard. *The Reformed Pastor.* 1656; Edinburgh: The Banner of Truth Trust, 1974.

Bridges, Charles. *The Christian Ministry; With an Inquiry into the Causes of Its Inefficiency; With an Especial Reference to the Ministry of the Establishment.* London: Seeley, 1849.

Brown, John. *The Christian Pastor's Manual.* Ligonier, 1826; Pennsylvania: Soli Deo Gloria, 1991.

Cameron, N.M. and S.B. Ferguson, *Pulpit and People: Essays in Honour of William Still on His 75th Birthday.* Edinburgh: Rutherford House Books, 1986.

Fairbairn, Patrick. *Pastoral Theology: A Treatise on the Office and Duties of the Christian Pastor.* 1875; Audubon, New Jersey: Old Paths Publications, 1992.

James, John Angell. *An Earnest Ministry: The Want of the Times.* 1847; Edinburgh: The Banner of Truth Trust, 1993.

Miller, Samuel. *Letters on Clerical Manners and Habits: Addressed to a Student in the Theological Seminary at Princeton, N.J.* Philadelphia: Presbyterian Board of Publications, 1852.

Murphy, Thomas. *Pastoral Theology: The Pastor in the Various Duties of His Office*. 1877; Audubon, New Jersey: Old Paths Publications, 1996.

Plummer, William S. *Hints & Helps in Pastoral Theology*. 1874; Harrisonburg, Virginia: Sprinkle Publications, 2003.

Porter, Ebenezer. *Lectures on Homilectics and Preaching, and on Public Prayer; Together with Sermons and Letters*. New York: Flagg, Gould and Newman, 1834.

Shedd, William G. T. *Homiletics and Pastoral Theology*. 1867; Edinburgh: The Banner of Truth Trust, 1965.

Spurgeon, C.H. *An All-Around Ministry: Addresses to Ministers and Students*. 1900; Edinburgh: The Banner of Truth Trust, 1965.

Spurgeon, C.H. *Lectures to My Students: A Selection from Addresses Delivered to the Student of The Pastors' College, Metropolitan Tabernacle*. 1881; Edinburgh, The Banner of Truth Trust, 2008.

Still, William. *The Work of the Pastor*. Fearn, Ross-shire: Christian Focus Publications, 2010.

## PUBLIC PRAYER

Henry, Matthew. *A Method for Prayer*. ed. J. Ligon Duncan, III. 1710; Fearn, Ross-shire: Christian Heritage, 1994.

MacLaren. *Public Prayers*. 1907; Grand Rapids, Michigan: Zondervan Publishing House, 1956.

Miller, Samuel. *Thoughts on Public Prayer*. 1849; Harrisonburg, Virginia: Sprinkle Publications, 1985.

Old, Hughes Oliphant. *Leading in Prayer: A Workbook for Ministers*. Grand Rapids, Michigan: William B. Eerdmans Publishing Company, 1995.

Old, Hughes Oliphant. "The Psalms as Christian Prayer. A Preface to the Liturgical Use of the Psalter." Unpublished manuscript, 1978.

Pratt, Richard. *Pray With Your Eyes Open*. Phillipsburg, NJ: Presbyterian and Reformed Pub. Co., 1987.

Robertson, O. Palmer. *A Way to Pray*. Edinburgh: Banner of Truth Trust, 2010.

Watts, Isaac. *A Guide to Prayer*. 1715; Edinburgh: Banner of Truth Trust, 2001.

## PREACHING

Adams, Jay E. *Preaching with Purpose*. Phillipsburg, New Jersey: Presbyterian and Reformed Publishing Company, 1982.

Alexander, James W. *Thoughts on Preaching: Being Contributions to Homiletics*. 1864; Edinburgh: The Banner of Truth Trust, 1975.

Broadus, John A. *On the Preparation and Delivery of Sermon*. 1870; Revised Edition, Nashville: Broadman Press, 1944.

Brooks, Phillips. *Lectures on Preaching Delivered before the Divinity School of Yale College In January and February, 1877*. New York: E. P. Dutton and Company, 1907.

Carrick, John. *The Imperative of Preaching: A Theology of Sacred Rhetoric*. Edinburgh: The Banner of Truth Trust, 2002.

Dabney, Robert L. *Sacred Rhetoric or A Course of Lectures on Preaching*. 1870; Edinburgh: The Banner of Truth Trust, 1979.

Dale, R.W. *Nine Lectures on Preaching*. London: Hodder and Stoughton, 1877.

Doddridge, Philip. *Lectures on Preaching*. London: R. Edwards, 1807.

Johnson, D. E. *Him We Proclaim: Preaching Christ from All the Scriptures*. Phillipsburg, New Jersey: P&R Publishing, 2007.

Lloyd-Jones, D. Martin. *Preaching and Preachers*. Grand Rapids, Michigan: Zondervan, 1971.

Logan, Jr., Samuel T. *The Preacher and Preaching: Reviving the Art in the Twentieth Century*. Phillipsburg, New Jersey: Presbyterian and Reformed Publishing Company, 1986.

Motyer, J. Alec. *Preaching? Simple Teaching on Simply Preaching*. Ross-shire, Scotland: Christian Focus Publications, 2013.

Old, Hughes O. *The Reading & Preaching of the Scriptures in the Worship of the Christian Church,* Vol. 1-8. Grand Rapids, Michigan: Eerdmans, 1998- (still in progress).

Perkins, William. *The Art of Prophesying with the Calling of the Ministry*. 1592, Edinburgh: The Banner of Truth Trust, 1982.

Robinson, Haddon W. *Biblical Preaching*. Grand Rapids: Baker Book House, 1980.

Stott, John R. W. *Between Two Worlds: The Art of Preaching in the Twentieth Century*. Grand Rapids, Michigan: William B. Eerdmans Publishing Company, 1982.

Willimon, William H. *Preaching and Leading Worship*. Philadelphia: The Westminster Press, 1984.

Also available from Christian Focus Publications ...

*Why we need the Church
(and why the Church needs us)*

# WHO NEEDS THE
# CHURCH?

## TERRY JOHNSON

978-1-5271-0835-6

# *Who Needs the Church?*

*Why We Need the Church (and Why the Church Needs Us)*

Terry L. Johnson

**A thought-provoking introduction to the importance of the local church.**

It seems that increasing numbers of professing Christians in the West do not attend church. Church, to many, has become a place to go when it is convenient, to have one's needs met. Terry L. Johnson asks whether our individualistic, dismissive attitude to the gathering of the local church can be squared with that of the New Testament.

Examining what the Bible has to say about the church, Johnson shows why the local body of believers is an essential part of the life of every believer – and the role that each individual believer plays in the life of the church. This thought–provoking, challenging book will benefit every believer.

*This book will not only enhance your growth in grace but will become an instrument as you disciple others in Christ's Church.*
— Harry L. Reeder III (1948–2023)

... a biblical yet practical resource to encourage family times together around the throne of grace

**H. B. CHARLES JR.**

# UNDERSTANDING
# FAMILY
# WORSHIP

## Its History, Theology and Practice

### TERRY L. JOHNSON

978-1-5271-0788-5

# Understanding Family Worship

*Its History, Theology and Practice*

Terry L. Johnson

**An enriching companion to Terry L. Johnson's popular** *Family Worship Book.*

The practice of family worship has been a foundation stone of faith for many families across many generations. In his book *The Family Worship Book*, Terry L. Johnson aided families to have meaningful times of devotion together. In this supplement to *The Family Worship Book*, Terry L. Johnson seeks to strengthen, clarify and enrich those devotions.

He begins by looking at the godly home, which provides the vital context in which family worship occurs. Then, the biblical and theological arguments for daily family worship are examined, drawing from the Old and New Testaments as well as the classic authors.

Once the case for family worship has been made, Johnson then moves on to develop the elements or practices which comprise family worship, as well as helpful tips for establishing the discipline practice of family worship. Finally, he discusses catechizing. Together, this monogram provides a feast of classic Reformed insight.

*This book will help you to deepen your understanding or sharpen your practice of family worship: Read it! Use it! Share it!.*

– H.B. Charles, Pastor-Teacher,
Shiloh Metropolitan Baptist Church, Jacksonville, Florida

# Christian Focus Publications

Our mission statement –

STAYING FAITHFUL
In dependence upon God we seek to impact the world through literature faithful to His infallible Word, the Bible. Our aim is to ensure that the Lord Jesus Christ is presented as the only hope to obtain forgiveness of sin, live a useful life and look forward to heaven with Him.

Our Books are published in four imprints:

CHRISTIAN
**FOCUS**

popular works including biographies, commentaries, basic doctrine and Christian living.

CHRISTIAN
**HERITAGE**

books representing some of the best material from the rich heritage of the church.

**MENTOR**

books written at a level suitable for Bible College and seminary students, pastors, and other serious readers. The imprint includes commentaries, doctrinal studies, examination of current issues and church history.

**CF4•K**

children's books for quality Bible teaching and for all age groups: Sunday school curriculum, puzzle and activity books; personal and family devotional titles, biographies and inspirational stories – because you are never too young to know Jesus!

Christian Focus Publications Ltd,
Geanies House, Fearn, Ross-shire,
IV20 1TW, Scotland, United Kingdom.
www.christianfocus.com